ELEANOR

PORTRAIT OF A FARJEON

Other Publications

FINDING MY WAY (Autobiography)
ADVICE TO A PLAYER
ACTING MY WAY

Poems

THE CHASTENING

Helen Craig

Eleanor Farjeon
in the studio room where all her work was done and where she
received all her friends and visitors

ELEANOR

PORTRAIT OF A FARJEON

by

DENYS BLAKELOCK

LONDON
VICTOR GOLLANCZ LTD
1966

PRINTED IN GREAT BRITAIN
BY EBENEZER BAYLIS AND SON, LTD.
THE TRINITY PRESS, WORCESTER, AND LONDON

In 'Forty-nine
A Curlew flew,
And there was I
And there were you.

Inscription by Eleanor Farjeon

AUTHOR'S NOTE

This book was written with Eleanor Farjeon's knowledge and with her co-operation in the verification of details, and in that she put all letters and poems concerning our friendship at my disposal, together with written permission to include them in this Memoir. The book, however, was not to be published during her lifetime.

ACKNOWLEDGMENTS

The Author wishes to acknowledge his indebtedness to the Oxford University Press for their permission to quote from *A Nursery in the Nineties*; and to Jonathan Cape Ltd., and Mrs. H. M. Davies for allowing him to make use of the poem, 'My Youth' from *The Complete Poems of W. H. Davies*.

The extract from Eleanor Farjeon's play, *The Silver Curlew*, is reproduced by kind permission of the publishers, Samuel French Ltd.

A*

AUTHOR'S FOREWORD

THIS BOOK HAS an unusual history. It was begun in the autumn of 1963, in Eleanor Farjeon's lifetime, put on one side and the blueprint taken up again in 1964, this time with Miss Farjeon's knowledge, blessing and approval.

She wanted not to read the manuscript because, she said, "I don't like seeing myself in the looking-glass." But she liked the idea of my writing the book, and thought well of the shape it was taking from what I told her from time to time. In fact, she brought all her usual enthusiasm to bear upon a project in which for once she could play no active part. On one occasion she went so far as to say, "I *am* enjoying being in on my obituary," and on another, "Splendid! Now all I have to do is to die." This sensible, realistic attitude was typical of the character which I hope will be revealed in these pages.

Eleanor Farjeon agreed, I think, that it was better for me to write this book while she was yet with us and while I could be detached, rather than wait until after her death, when anything I wrote might be sentimentalised or put out of focus by the inevitable sadness of loss and separation.

The book was intended in the first place to be nothing more than a brief Memoir: a sketch, a portrait by someone who happened to be in a unique position to put it on to canvas.

However, after I had sent off to the typist a draft as final as it could be at that premature moment, the sudden discovery of many letters and poems I had received from Eleanor Farjeon over the years completely altered the situation. I knew then that I must write a different and fuller kind of book. This idea was fortified by Eleanor's suggestion that she should lend me all my side of our correspondence, which consisted of a great number of letters.

As far as I myself am concerned it is no part of my intention to write my own autobiography. My wish is to include only those personal details that may help to make the picture of Eleanor Farjeon's remarkable character as true and complete as it can be.

I hope to keep my own letters down to a minimum; and in many cases to quote extracts rather than the letters entire. In fact to regard them as having the same importance as a 'cue' to another actor's lines; a spotlight to pin-point the leading player's face, or illuminate a particular area of the scene.

D.B.

CHAPTER ONE

"HARRY-NELLIE-JOE-AND-BERTIE . . . Bertie died first, didn't he?"

"Yes, in 1945. We buried him on V Day . . . Harry in 1948; and Joe in 1955."

"And then there was one." I held my hand out to Eleanor across the kitchen table where we always fed. She took it and said, "Yes. But, like Wordsworth's child, I still say, 'We are four'."

And so she did. They were always immensely alive in her mind, those brothers of Nellie's. She was not half-Jewish for nothing. Her passion for 'Family' was intense. Those who have read *A Nursery in the Nineties* (or *Portrait of a Family* as it was called in America) will realise that she had cause to be proud of her family: her grandfather, the great American actor Joseph Jefferson; her father, a novelist and journalist of considerable standing. And her brothers? Harry, a musical genius, teacher at the Royal Academy of Music, of Solomon and of many others now famous in the world of music; Herbert (Bertie), Shakespeare scholar and the wittiest of lyricists and writers of revues, with a classical knowledge that gave his work a lasting quality; and Joe—Jefferson Farjeon, who made more money than any of them with his thrillers in play and book form.

Nellie, the most widely gifted, outlived them all; but the

four lived on in her. 'We're Harry-Nellie-Joe-and-Bertie.'
This family password was an outward sign of their inward
solidarity. Everywhere she went she spoke of them. Everything she wrote of any personal nature had to include those
names.

★

The title of this Memoir was deliberately chosen because
I knew that the subject would herself have approved of it, as
indeed she did when I told her of my choice. She liked the
name Eleanor and was pleased when people called her by it.
She was mainly known as Nellie by her family, and by those
friends who had first met her through her brother Bertie. I
seldom called her anything but Eleanor for years, until in
later times I would occasionally slip into Nellie or Nell (she
preferred Nell) in moments of banter or of special affection.

When one comes to work on a portrait of one's best and
most intimate woman friend, with a sincere desire that the
picture shall be a loving but a true one, the inevitable
question arises: 'How much shall I say?'

Nothing would be easier than to set down everything; to
put such a quantity of detail on the canvas that the eye would
be so preoccupied with it that the essential personality of the
subject would be lost.

In my portrait I am anxious to paint the real person, which
is something more than just the real personality. For a personality can be a mere public persona, that façade which we
all put up in order to be what the world expects of us. The
shedding of this persona and the release of true personality is,

perhaps, one of the most important objectives of every serious-thinking man and woman.

Eleanor Farjeon was eminently serious-minded, and she was the nearest to being a completely real person of anyone I have known; but even she, I think, was capable of assuming a persona, though perhaps unconsciously.

It would be easy to present a sentimental Victorian oleograph and call it *Nellie of the Nineties*. But I should not want to do that; and Eleanor, the woman who wrote *A Nursery in the Nineties*, who *was* a Victorian and was sentimental, but was so many other things besides, would not, I am sure, have wished me to do so.

This is not a life of Eleanor Farjeon, for so much has been written about her by herself and by others that such a work would seem redundant. It is, as I have said, a portrait: a Memoir, by one who, for the end period of her life, shared with her a very close, special and important relationship—one that was, or seemed to be, unique; a marriage of two minds, with mine as the weaker and less well-endowed partner. As close as that of husband and wife without the physical intimacies; spirit answering to spirit without the sometimes falsifying elements of romantic love.

It is for this reason that, though there are many qualified to write a better book about Eleanor Farjeon, I feel myself best fitted to write the truest.

★

When I met Eleanor in 1949 I was still a working actor and remained so until, in 1954, insuperable difficulties of health drove me out of the theatre. During those intervening years, although I spent every week-end and much of the week time too up at Eleanor's Hampstead home, going about with her to theatres and parties and visiting mutual friends, I went on living in my flat in Bloomsbury. Even after I left the stage I continued to keep my home in central London.

I would think I knew Eleanor better even than Pod did—her beloved Pod (George Earle) with whom she had lived for round about thirty years. I never met him, but from all I have learned about him from Eleanor, I have a picture in my mind of Pod as a brilliant scholar and teacher; but a man who lived, latterly at any rate, in a cocoon of contentment, immersed in a world of poesy and carpentry. He loved Keats passionately and worshipped wood, out of which he made with exquisite precision many beautiful things which were part of Eleanor's daily domestic life. Casual tables, tea caddies, table lamps and endless shelves to take the steadily increasing number of books of every description. Eleanor has described him as being 'drenched' in poetry. The beauty of the English language was one of the many bonds between them.

He respected and took pleasure in her first-class brain, her wide general knowledge, and the facility with which she solved the intricacies of the *Times* crossword puzzle.

As to her relationship with Pod, it must be remembered that Eleanor had not been brought up to practise the Jewish Faith of her father. Nor was she until 1953—nominally—a Christian; although I think it would be no over-statement to describe her as the most Christlike character I have ever met. And it is strange and interesting that, years before she was baptised a Christian and a Catholic, she had written *Ten Saints*, countless carols, and much verse of a religious nature.

In view of her lack of any orthodox convictions, when Eleanor agreed to live with Pod there was never any question for her of it being non-moral. She loved him with 'the holiness of the heart's affections', and to her there could be nothing wrong or unbeautiful about their relationship.

Eleanor told me more than once that she went to great pains to make quite sure that Pod's marriage was broken beyond hope of repair before she took this step. She would have been incapable of taking a man away from another woman in any circumstances. It just was not in Eleanor to snatch her own happiness at the expense of another's.

I have said that I believe I would have known Eleanor better even than Pod did, because he was not, as I think I have shown, an analytical man, which I am. I do not think he would have noticed idiosyncrasies of character. It would not have been part of him to observe with detachment Eleanor's fascinating traits and many inconsistencies.

It remains, therefore, for me to put my analytical training and my actor's powers of observation to the good purpose of presenting Eleanor's character and personality as they emerge through the story of our friendship.

CHAPTER TWO

WHEN ELEANOR FARJEON and I met in 1949 it was in fact a re-meeting. We had become acquainted ten years before that, when I appeared for a few weeks in *An Elephant in Arcady*, the light opera written by Eleanor and Herbert Farjeon which I hope will one day be revived. And we had run into each other once since then, in 1945, when I was in *Lady Windermere's Fan* at the Haymarket. I remember her telling me she had seen the original production in 1892. She was then only eleven years old, but she could remember vividly Marion Terry's first entrance as Mrs. Erlynne in the ballroom scene.

But it was not until November 1949 that my friendship with Eleanor really began. The Arts Theatre management were preparing, as a Christmas entertainment, her piece, *The Silver Curlew*, a play for children of all ages. They asked me if I would take the part of King Nollekens of Norfolk. 'We think it's time you played a King,' they said. I thought perhaps it was time too, and play him I did, cardboard crown, gilded sceptre and all.

Nollekens (Nolly for short) was a cry-baby King of indeterminate age, who went about with his Nanny, and had a double nature of which he was inordinately proud.

NOLLEKENS: I can't help it Nanny . . . I've got a double
        nature.

NANNY: So's everybody.

NOLLEKENS: Not as double as mine. When I'm good I'm *very* very good.

NANNY: When you are bad . . .

NOLLEKENS: Yes, I'm horrid.

When he was horrid he would stamp his foot and cry and chop off people's heads, which delighted the children in the audience. The character of Nollekens was beautifully drawn and represented the childlike element which remains in most of us all our lives. Eleanor always used to say she might have written the rôle especially for me. She soon got to know that I too had a double nature. Unlike the dual personality in her, of which I shall be writing later and which was productive of only good for all who knew her, my duality caused distress to those around me, as well as being destructive to myself and my career.

There is a short undated letter written to Eleanor by me in the early days of our friendship:

So sorry, darling. Please forgive me. But you see I *have* got a double nature!

The only difference between Nollekens and me was that he was proud of his double nature and I detested mine. My life was a constant struggle to bring these two warring halves together, and no one did more to help me in the painful process of integration than Eleanor, with her love and gentleness, her wisdom and her patience.

It was no capricious chance that brought us together for the rehearsals of *The Silver Curlew*. We were both in need,

Eleanor as much as I; for less than two weeks before we met she had lost the man with whom she had shared her life for the last thirty years. George Earle, her beloved Pod, had died on November 12th, 1949.

Round about the time of our meeting a friend of mine said to me, "Eleanor Farjeon's influence must be very good for you. She's so cheerful."

The friend was right, and she chose the word to describe exactly Eleanor's sunny nature and its calming influence. She was great fun. Apart from her gift for making Christmas and every birthday something very special, just in the ordinary way of things she had her own unique touch with which she lightened the humdrum and the commonplace and put one's darkest fears to rest. This meant much to me, for by that time I had allowed fear to gain a stranglehold on me and depressions to dominate my days and nights.

Never did I appreciate this side of her character as much as I did then, during the rehearsals of *The Silver Curlew*. I had made a very shaky start and, in fact, did my utmost to withdraw from the engagement, a thing I was guilty of doing all too frequently in my professional life in the theatre. Eleanor did her successful best to make the ways as smooth for me as possible, with her gay spirit and her genius for organising and dealing with the problems of creature comforts and anticipating one's every need.

"This is the Perrin's Walk Catering Department," she would cry down the telephone without preamble. That was an offer to bring thermoses of coffee and sandwiches to rehearsal. She knew that I leaned on these things at that time, but was too disorientated to prepare them before the day's work. Or, "This is the Perrin's Walk Electrical Engineering Department," when the heating in my dressing-room had broken down. An electric fire, bought in Hampstead, was on its way for the evening performance. Or, "This is the Perrin's Walk Domestic Agency." When I was in urgent need for someone to come and put my flat to rights Eleanor even lent me her 'Mrs. Mopp' for an hour or two and made all arrangements for her to arrive safely.

It will be easy to see from these few instances alone that Eleanor, to anyone given as I was to states of anxiety and agitation, was the perfect figure of security, strong, reassuring and dependable.

One of her early visits to my flat happened to fall on a Friday. To make things simpler for me she had offered to bring a picnic lunch. I reminded her of the fact that as I was a Catholic it had to be a meatless day. The next morning I had a card from her. On it was written:

Tomorrow

> I'll be there
> With Friday fare;
> Things in tins
> That once had fins,
> Cheese and eggs—
> But nothing with legs;
> And none of the things
> That once had wings.

ELEANOR

Written for Denys Blakelock
on a Thursday and a post card,
accepting an invitation to a meal.

★

What a Christmas it was, that year at the Arts Theatre! Eleanor was in and out of the dressing-rooms with presents and 'a happy Christmas' for everyone, the perfect Fairy Godmother as usual and, as always, adored by every member of the large Company. Theatre people are particularly responsive to friendliness and affection, and Eleanor distributed hers without favouritism or consideration of seniority or status. No one could ever be left out if Eleanor had anything to do with it. And how she enjoyed it all—every rehearsal and every evening performance—with the eagerness of a child at a party. This does not mean to say that the grown-up Eleanor was not acutely aware of everything that went on in the way of hard work on the production; or that she did not bring into the theatre those professional standards of perfection that she applied to every aspect of her writing.

I was never good at making speeches, but on the first night of *The Silver Curlew* I did make one. There was something quite exceptional in the volume and quality of the applause that burst out at the mention of the author's name. I realised that here was a woman who was not only admired and respected as an artist, but also greatly loved as a human being. In fact, I was so thrown by this that to my shame I forgot to mention Clifton Parker, whose score was such an adornment to the play.

22

I saw Eleanor almost every evening at the theatre and generally she gave me a lift home in the car that came to fetch her. Life was too busy for both of us during that successful Christmas season for me to get up to Hampstead to see her home. All that was to come later. When the play came to an end I went Bunburying in Hertfordshire for two weeks, and it wasn't until the middle of February that I paid my first visit to the house that was going to play such a big part in my life for many years to come.

CHAPTER THREE

IT WAS ALWAYS my custom to go away for a week or two if possible after I finished an engagement. (This strikes a strange note of leisureliness compared with the conditions now obtaining in the theatre.) So, as soon as *The Silver Curlew* finished, I went down to Harpenden to stay, as I often did, with an old friend of ours, Mrs. Spencer Pickering, in her Elizabethan farmhouse, The Granary.

It was while I was there that my correspondence with Eleanor Farjeon began. Nothing, perhaps, advances a relationship more quickly than an exchange of letters between two people who find themselves on the threshold of a new and important friendship.

Eleanor and I had been immediately drawn together from that first afternoon rehearsal of *The Silver Curlew*. She saw at once that there was something amiss, that I was suffering under some kind of emotional *crise*; and her immediate response and sympathy, so typical of Eleanor, did much to relieve the situation. I was struck by the complete unselfishness of her attitude. The interest of the play meant everything to her, especially at that moment of bereavement in her life. It could have entailed a great deal of money too. (I was not to know then how little monetary considerations counted where Eleanor was concerned.) She wanted me for this important part, for which I was particularly suited, and here was I trying to back out of it. Yet her only thought was for me, a comparative stranger, a mere acquaintance. I must do exactly what I felt to be wisest and happiest for myself, she said. If the nervous strain was going to be too much, I must unhesitatingly withdraw. There was nothing of the ruthless creative artist about Eleanor Farjeon. For her the human side was always the thing that came foremost. She would even risk having her work disturbed rather than make herself immune from interruptions, or ever be not available to someone who might be in need of her.

There was one thing that Eleanor could not know at that time. The fact of her making it so easy for me to escape had the psychological effect of making me feel less committed. John Fernald, too, the producer of the play, supported her in this. His extraordinary understanding, commonsense and kindness, coupled with Eleanor's unselfishness, all helped to harden my resolve to go on with the job and carry it through.

How true it is that our fate lies 'not in our stars but in ourselves'. If, on that occasion, I had not gone on with it and had given up my part in *The Silver Curlew*, a great friendship would have died before it had begun, and many other lives would have been affected and would have taken a quite different direction.

While I was writing this book I confessed to Eleanor that the memory of that first year of our friendship was a little hazy. "What were we doing in 1950?" I asked her. She reminded me of isolated episodes and then she added, "And—getting to know each other." Now, after so many years, I find it difficult to picture a time when I knew her less well than I

did at the period when this conversation took place. But a
great friendship of that kind, however spontaneous and immediate in its beginnings, must take time to come to its full
flowering.

Getting to know each other. Certainly there was much to
explore in Eleanor's many-sided character. As for me, it was
now that she began to discover by slow degrees the complicated human being whom she had taken into her life.

In late January 1950, down at Harpenden, with all the
problems and excitements of the play behind me, I wrote my
first letter to Eleanor from The Granary. On my arrival I had
found one from her awaiting me, as I always did wherever I
went from then onwards.

Unfortunately, I have always had a mania for clearing out
drawers and getting rid of papers. As a result of this I was
dismayed, on going through the correspondence between
Eleanor Farjeon and myself, to find that I had kept only
certain special letters I received from her and none that were
dated earlier than 1951; which means that readers of this book
will have to see Eleanor writing to me as it were in a looking-
glass; to imagine the kind of letters she wrote in the early
days of our friendship, from the reflection shown in mine.

This is what I replied in answer to that first letter I found
waiting for me at Harpenden:

Thursday, January 26, 1950

You really are a wonderful person. As I believe I told
you, you do help me to see God more clearly; and to
realise something of how wonderful He must be, if He can

create a human being as good and kind and warm and generous and loving as you are.

It was good of you to think of sending me a letter to greet me here and it was a great joy to see it sitting there when I arrived. And then, after tea, up in my room, looking out across the frozen fields, to open it and find that enchanting holy picture of 'le Presentation' (or la?).

You really are a fairy after all. You not only appear at the right moment always, but you also bring in your hand the right thing to fit the occasion, conjured out of some secret magic hoard of your own.

. . .

On February 13th [Eleanor's birthday] I am happy to think that I will be able to make up to you a bit for the loss you might otherwise have felt more keenly on that day of the year. I've been very self-centred with you so far but I do really feel the greatest interest in and concern for my friends, and was glad you told me more the other day.

I do hope you weren't, by any chance, being taken already to the Globe? If so, please tell me and I will get the business manager to change the seats for another day. For the rest, what would you like? Would you care to have a *cosy* tea in HIS ROOMS at about 4? Or what would you like? It's your day.

The reference to the Globe concerned *Ring Round the Moon*. I had booked seats on the chance for Eleanor's birthday. And there will be several allusions to HIS ROOMS. That was our name for my flat. The joke derived from the stock phrase of Victorian and Edwardian novels: SHE WAS COM-PROMISED by being seen visiting HIS ROOMS. Lady Windermere's visit to Lord Darlington's apartment in *Lady Windermere's Fan* is a good example of this.

It is quite certain that I had a letter from Eleanor in answer to mine very soon; and my reply to it shows fairly plainly the sort of letter it was and the kind of things she wrote about.

Weds. Feb. 1st, 1950

What wonderful letters you do write: but I suppose I ought not to be surprised at that. Anyhow, thank you for another one, which amongst other things made me laugh a great deal. . . .

About the Globe: it's not really surprising that I should have asked; because, when you've known someone for 35 years (skipped) and three months, you detect the subtle changes of tone and tempo—even on the telephone. I felt there was something at the back of your voice, but couldn't place what it could be till afterwards.

I *am* sorry you've seen it before; but as it seems to have delighted you so much, and as I take it you will always tell me the complete truth about everything, I must believe that it will really give you pleasure to go a second time with me, and I shall look forward to it enormously.

I, being I, like gangway seats (though I *can* sit 3 or 4 seats away from it) but was unable to get 3rd or 4th row. So I had to take the front row. I hope you won't mind this—I love it, but most people don't.

Also, I'm not fond of 'going round' to see people; but in this case, Paul Scofield is very much on my conscience, and I would like to take the opportunity and will write before and tell him we are coming. Unless you'd hate this. Will you tell me?

And will you tell me, too, if SHE likes her cavalier to dress for the theatre? I never do, but I think I know where my dinner jacket might be. Probably if I wore a dark, 'gentlemanly' suit, and you got into a 'low blouse', we might not disgrace ourselves. What do you think?

Do you notice I haven't used one exclamation mark?

(I was beginning to learn things from Eleanor about the craft of writing and book-making. It was at this time that the first seeds were planted of my small gift for writing, which was to reveal itself later on and the development of which was to make such a difference to both our lives.)

. . . Now it is after tea-time, and I'm going to finish and post this tomorrow. Yet another nice letter from my dear Eleanor this morning—thank you, oh, thank you—and for the charming legend and poem of St. Bridget. I had seen neither before or even heard of the legend.

I do like your Missal. When mine comes, I will show it to you and how it works. I suppose Missal means just 'Mass-book'; for that is its main purpose—to set out the special Mass for each day of the year. They are printed for Catholics in Latin on one side, and in the language of the country on the other; but the Priest always and everywhere says the Mass in Latin. So you get the Mass being offered all over the world in a universal tongue; and pronounced in the way Italian is spoken.

Talking of all this, how happy and touched I am to know that you hold the little blue rosary in your hand at night. . . .

The query as to what would be *comme il faut* in the way of dress for the stalls of the Globe Theatre strikes a period note now; and talk of the Latin Mass, with the vernacular translation alongside, seems to belong to another age.

Eleanor's mention of holding the little blue rosary in her hand at night reminds me that Jimmie (James) Roose Evans warned her about this at the time. "You're playing with dynamite, you know." She was—as will be seen.

Eleanor continued to sleep with a rosary in her hand to the last day of her life, but they got larger with the years. The definitive rosary was enormous—the biggest I have ever seen. Each bead was the size of a small marble. She loved it and it suited her. Eleanor never did things by halves.

Here is another letter written from the Granary:

February 7, St. Romauld 1950

That was a very beautiful letter you wrote to me—and very funny too. That's what I like about you specially; and that's what I like about the Catholic Faith—the mixture of grave and gay.

I loved all you said about the other side of the door— I'm there too—and I couldn't tell you at what particular moment I found myself there. I only know that the door must have begun to open on that horrible afternoon, in that terrible rehearsal room, and continued in the snack-bar; when, in the middle of my own dark troubles, I was so amazed to hear such completely unselfish assurances coming from someone who, up till three hours previously, had been little more than an acquaintance. And on we went from there. . . . But as you say, we won't dissect.. . . . I *am* looking forward to NEXT MONDAY. Tea at 4—carriages, or rather HIS BROUGHAM, at 6.45. The rest to be arranged on Sunday morning—or Saturday evening. Perhaps SHE'd like to come back to HIS ROOMS for a glass of something and to say good-night . . . . Meanwhile have a lovely week at Oxford.

God bless you my dearest Eleanor. Thank you for your last little Saint—and thank you for helping, with your letters, to make the holiday I was rather dreading such a happy one. Post no letters here after Wednesday. . . .

One important thing happened while I was down at Harpenden. It was there that I planned and bought my first birthday present for Eleanor. Her day was then approaching, February 13th.

I had recently read in her Nursery book the touching story of a disappointment she had suffered as a child at a Christmas party. When it came to presents from the Christmas tree, little Nellie had her eye on a fascinating writing-case. Sure enough, when her turn came, the lady who was handing out the presents gave the coveted case to Nellie, whose excitement was as intense as only a child's can be. But as she moved away, the lady called out she was sorry but she was afraid

that she had made a mistake. The writing-case belonged to
another little girl. It was taken away from Nellie, who was
given instead a calendar decorated with coloured ribbons.
Eleanor's account of this episode in *A Nursery in the Nineties*,
of her woeful disappointment, and of the complete spoiling
of the party, had moved me very much; and when later I
came to think about her birthday present this story gave me
an inspiration.

I made a happy discovery. In an antique shop at Harpenden
I found a writing-case in jade green leather embroidered with
gold. I took it to a stationer's and had it stuffed to the seams
with pens, pencils and nibs, ribbons and rubbers, paper and
envelopes, sealing-wax, drawing-pins—I can remember no
more. But there was nothing left out which could delight
the heart of a small Victorian girl. Among our correspondence I found this brief undated note that I enclosed in the
parcel:

> Good morning, dear, dear Eleanor: and a very, very
> happy birthday and many many happy returns.
> This is the case you *didn't* have from that Christmas tree
> in the 90's—with some of the things that you would have
> filled it with.

This time the Victorian child was not disappointed. I am
sure that nothing I ever thought of for Eleanor in later years
gave her as much pleasure as that first birthday present. It was
with a slightly damp eye that I heard her recount this episode
many years afterwards in a talk on Children's Hour.

CHAPTER FOUR

BY FEBRUARY 13TH, Eleanor's sixty-ninth birthday, I was
back in London and was preparing to welcome her at HIS
ROOMS. SHE had been there once before on the last night of
The Silver Curlew. She had given me a lift home as usual and
had come in for a drink. I had still not yet seen Eleanor's
house in Hampstead.

I do not remember very much about the birthday afternoon but the memory of the evening at the Globe Theatre is
a vivid one. It was the first play we had seen together.
Anouilh's *Ring Round the Moon* was the sort of occasion one
does not forget, and our visit to Paul Scofield afterwards in
his dressing-room was a complete success. It would be difficult to imagine anyone who would not take to Scofield. He
is as warm and friendly and modest today as he was then,
when he was beginning to come into his own as an important
actor.

The birthday was over and Eleanor, with her special
capacity for enjoyment, had loved every moment of it, from
the time when the first telephone bell rang and the usual
shower of presents and flowers and telegrams had begun to
pour into Perrin's Walk, to the moment after the theatre
when she dropped me at my flat and we said goodnight.

All that Eleanor had learned about me during the rehearsals of *The Silver Curlew* and through our exchange of letters

while I was away was only the beginning of the ramifications that revealed themselves as the months passed by, as will be seen from these extracts from letters written by me at this early stage of our friendship.

. . . Yes—God and the Devil—good and evil. Catholics believe in a positive and personal devil, you know, And I've always had a feeling that he made a special target of me. (Unless I'm flattering myself.) Certainly my life has been a very marked struggle between a desire for great good and a propensity for great evil. . . . How clearly you see that light and darkness, shadow and sunlight, have a very special significance for me. . . .

This was no exaggeration, no self-dramatisation on my part. It was plain fact; and it seemed that it all began half a century earlier when, as a small child, I was staying, as I often did, in my grandmother's home, Paston House in Cambridge. Aladdin's cave could not have been more intriguing to him than the inside of Paston House was to me, with its dark, shadowy hall and tall, winding staircase; its long, mysterious corridors, innumerable rooms and unexpected corners to be explored. I remember the large drawing-room on the ground floor, with its many French windows opening on to the lawn, and at night-time the huge glittering chandelier which made everything downstairs seem cheerful and friendly.

But by day or by night, up there at the top of the stairs at the end of a long passage, there was something I did not like. I knew what it was but I could not talk about it then. My grandmother was there and she was not alone. She was ill and helpless and in the power of Someone—Someone I hated and who hated me: tall, dark, forbidding, and I was frightened; frightened but fascinated too.

There was one particular period at Paston House which left an indelible imprint on my mind. I had some serious illness and was left behind, this hated person, who was in fact my grandmother's nurse, in charge, while my parents and all the family returned to London. Suddenly everything was changed. Gone were the familiar faces, the friendly voices, the excitement and the bustle I had known. I only was there, up at the top of that now sinister house, alone and helpless in a darkened room in the power of that inimical personality. No Babylonian captive could have felt more desolate than I did then. The waters of separation flowed over me, a blanket of impenetrable melancholy came down upon me and I could do nothing.

Although in the light of cold adult reasoning it is easy now to dispel the shadows of that fantasy world, nevertheless there was certainly plenty of material there for a child's mind to build upon. And I have no doubt that it was in that house and at this period that I acquired my exaggerated fear of darkness and of being shut in; of being cut off from those I love and from safe, familiar ground; of being immobilised and helpless; and of being in any way under compulsion or duress.

All these interrelated fears were to have an important bearing on the things that happened to me many years later. They were the direct cause of the claustrophobia with which I have had to reckon ever since those days. This nervous symptom is a thing that is understood by most normal people to some extent, but only those who have had to deal with it as an acute illness in themselves or in someone close to them can know how far-reaching and destructive its effects can be. I myself have not been in an underground railway since I was twenty. I cannot remember when it was that I gave up going in lifts; to this day I choose to climb eight floors to the big studio at the top of Broadcasting House rather than take the elevator.

This situation, though unpleasant, was quite manageable before the war. But the black-out, gas masks, underground shelters, and the conditions of every kind of transport under warfare only served to exacerbate these fears in the unconscious, and to make life very involved indeed. Nor has the return of the so-called peace done anything to restore my morale as to mobility, with the congestion on the roads now as well as on the railways.

There was an amusing cartoon in a newspaper during the war: a drawing of two cows descending side by side from a cattle-truck on to the platform. One was saying to the other, "My dear, it was disgraceful. We were herded together just like human beings."

Three weeks after war was declared I returned from Devonshire, where I had been convalescing from a serious physical illness. That unforgettable journey in a packed railway carriage gave me an early foretaste of what train travel was going to be like under the circumstances of air raids and overcrowding.

The first thing I did on getting to London was to buy a

bicycle. This solved some of my problems for the duration of the war, but only local ones confined to London. As far as journeys of any distance were concerned, I soon found myself compelled to give up going in railway trains as I had had to give up the Tube twenty years before; and to rail travel I have never returned.

The Army Medical Board rejected me outright on account of the psychological history. I was put into Grade 4 and spent the war doing my own professional work in the theatre. Unfortunately this had become a very limited field of employment for anyone placed as I was. All the plays were being sent out on long provincial tours, impossible for me because of the train travel they necessitated, and if one could not take part in the preliminary tour, neither could one appear in the London production.

But this difficulty of transport and its effect on my professional activities was not the only handicap that caused the confusion in my circumstances. There had been for many years another complication, even more serious in its nature, although it also had its roots in the claustrophobic element. I had had a strictly religious upbringing by my father, a clergyman, himself the son of a stern Victorian parson, which had left me with a highly-trained, not to say over-developed, conscience about sex. The effect of this on a strongly-sexed young man whose daily terror was to be shut in, to be inhibited or frustrated in any way, proved to be disastrous. In the end the unremitting conflict was so great that it brought about the ruin of a successful career.

It was hardly to be wondered at that by the time Eleanor

Farjeon and I met up with one another I, approaching forty-nine, was an established victim of dark moods of depression and anxiety, and subject to irrational fits of anger and resentments.

There is a letter written by Eleanor in the fourth year of our friendship which I feel could well be included here, since this is not a day to day journal, but the portrait of a personality as seen through its overall effect on another human being throughout a prolonged period. Moreover, this particular letter refers back to a revealing episode which took place in the phase of which I am now writing:

Jan. 27th 1954

What a specially lovely teatime-and-after it was, in your room where the things you have got together there are richer for your choosing them with so much liking, and where the richest thing of all is what you can show your friend without ever seeing it yourself—your own face quiet and happy in its setting. When you asked me yesterday if I remembered your weeping in that chair (as if I could forget) it was like a picture out of the past—I sat on the chair-arm, holding you, with your dear face bowed into your hands and the tears trickling through the fingers, while you whispered, "I feel so dried up." You have come a long way since then, darling, into a prospect of happiness out of one of sorrow. You did have bursts of happiness that relieved the sorrow, and you will have, no doubt, moods of sorrow to shadow the happiness—we are all so full of weather, it can hardly be otherwise—but oh the difference in your outlook, under any sky! (yes, even if presently you are asking me to begin the Thirty Days again). I have never felt you, in your own place, quite as I did yesterday. I came home so happy—

> "To what a height my spirit is contending!
> 'Tis not content so soon to be alone"—

Only, as Keats knew very well, one's spirit is not alone after being with its friends. We can't regret even the sorrow of a friend if—as we said yesterday—it took down the gate and gave us the freedom of him, as your sorrow and pain gave you to me, as my sorrow and emptiness gave me to you. When friends have entered that part of each other completely, we cannot come out from it alone as we were before, for he whom we entered is now some of oneself. And that is why, I believe, we must enter Christ through His Passion; it is only after we have been with Him in Gethsemane that we can have Him in Heaven. I can't regret whatever humble reflection of Gethsemane here has been mine through suffering, and still less (because you are more to me than myself) can I regret yours for you. Not after seeing you yesterday smiling in the chair where I saw you weep.

. . .

The reference in Eleanor's letter to the possibility of my asking her to 'begin the Thirty Days again' should be explained, as the Thirty Days played an important part in our lives and will appear more than once in later letters.

The Thirty Days Prayer is a devotion well known amongst

39

certain sorts of Catholics. It takes its name from the fact that it has to be recited for a period of thirty days. It is addressed to Our Lady and is said to be especially efficacious, as indeed I found it to be whenever Eleanor said it for my intention. The merit acquired for reciting such a prayer even once should be considerable. It is very long, taking about a quarter of an hour to get through. It is involved and cumbersome, in a flowery translation from the French; the word 'aimable', for instance, being rendered into English as 'aimiable'. The idea of Eleanor Farjeon, a poet and a lover of good prose, toiling through this act of devotion however tired she might be, to bring spiritual succour to her friend is touching indeed. No wonder her prayers were so often answered; and in the end it almost ceased to be a toil for her, or even an onslaught on her aesthetic sense. She used to say she had become quite attached to the Thirty Days Prayer; and, provided she had the book on her knees with which to prompt herself if necessary, she could say almost the whole of it by heart.

I alas! never had the will-power to do the same for her in return. The most I was ever able to offer in later years for Eleanor's special needs was the Memorare, a beautiful prayer, pleasant and easy to say—and very short:

Memorare

Remember, O most gracious Virgin Mary,
that never was it known that anyone who fled
to thy protection, implored thy help, or
sought thy intercession was left unaided.

Inspired with this confidence I fly unto thee,
O Virgin of Virgins, my mother. To thee I
come, before thee I stand, sinful and sorrowful.
O Mother of the Word Incarnate, despise not my
petitions, but in thy mercy hear and answer me.

Even Eleanor, in her later and wearier days, took to this as
a suitable substitute for the Thirty Days Prayer, though she
was still capable of saying that if she thought the need great
enough; and in fact said it last for me only five months before
she died.

In view of all that has been shown of Eleanor Farjeon's
great capacity for giving in this way, week in week out over
fifteen years, is it to be wondered at that so many of my
letters to her were written in a strain of reiterated love and
gratitude?

30 March 1950

What a more-than-welcome letter that was that came to
me from Perrin's Walk this morning.

It deserves a little reply—and it shall have it.

Dear Ellie—I wish I could tell you what a difference
you've made to my life. You've given me what I believe
has been your desire to give me—a feeling of real security.
The feeling of there being someone there in the background on whom I can always count, always depend in all
circumstances; who will always understand all things,
believe all things, accept all things—will never *mis*understand, never be hurt or take offence, or make demands to
which one cannot rise.

ELEANOR

And all this from someone whose dear affection is truly welcome to me and in whose company I can really delight. Thank you, thank you, thank you, dearest Ellie.

CHAPTER FIVE

OFTEN IN THE weeks since Christmas I had written Eleanor's address:

> 20 Perrin's Walk,
> Hampstead,
> N.W.3.

But now the moment had come to make the ascent to London's most select suburb and pay a call on her.

Ironically, the first visit was not altogether happy. It was a cold, rainy, February day and it so happened that it was one of my less good ones. My immediate reaction to Eleanor's house could not have been other than favourable, although it must have been too wet and cold for me to see the garden and the Garden Room. If I did I do not remember doing so. But on that occasion I do recollect that when I put my feet up on that well-used sofa in front of the fire I was conscious of everything being strangely dark. I soon realised that there was a huge screen, shutting in the sofa from the draught coming up from the staircase, which gave me a very enclosed feeling.

So much has been written about Eleanor's house in Perrin's Walk (once 'Church' Walk and changed, much to her disgust). It undoubtedly had great charm and originality, like so many old places that have been converted bit by bit over the years. Most people found it fascinating. But as far as I was concerned, although the whole place with its many associations came to mean a great deal to me, it was nevertheless a compliment to Eleanor and our friendship that with my special difficulties I was able to be happy in spending so much time in that particular house; for, despite all its charm, it had for me many drawbacks.

Once a coach-house belonging to one of the aristocratic residences in Church Row, it had been made over many years before into a painter's studio above, and a garage below. Gradually Eleanor had acquired the entire premises, with its old-fashioned little garden at the back with apple-trees bending to the ground. Over the whole leaned protectingly an ancient sycamore which to Eleanor's sorrow had eventually to be cut down for reasons of security. I shared her love for it and used to look up at it from my bed in the corner of the sitting-room, as this poem, The Sycamore Tree, will show:

> Through the skylight
> I see above me gleaming
> Moonshine on the leaves
> Of the sycamore tree;
> And to my seeming
> A fathering figure
> There it stands,
> Watching through the night
> With arms protecting,
> A blessing in its hands.
>
> Night past and day begun

I wake and through the skylight
See the leaves shining
In the tender sun.
Still that figure
Benign, paternal stands,
Giving shelter from daytime heat,
Shading me with cool, green hands.

Oh, ancient sycamore,
Into your ancestral branches,
In another land,
One who was small of stature
Climbed to see
Him who shades the unprotected
With a mighty hand,
And through the fiercest day
And darkest sleeping
Blesses me.

When the tree was cut down the skylight looked cold and bare. The magic had gone, and Eleanor could never speak about the sycamore again.

She had also been able to buy, through a happy accident, another larger piece of garden with a big tool-shed, that was adjacent to her property, separated by a right-of-way. The whole area was like a corner of Devon or Somerset, and was a wonderful retreat for me, cloistered as I was in a stuffy, one-roomed Bloomsbury flat. I dearly loved the garden and the charming Garden Room, into which the tool-shed had by then been converted.

But, unlike other people, I never felt quite happy about Eleanor's house, unusual and attractive though it was. The combination of sloping roofs and sunlessness gave to me a feeling of darkness and confinement. The sun shone only on the front rooms: Eleanor's bedroom, which she alone frequented, and the front downstairs dining-room which was scarcely used by anyone.

The kitchen, where we invariably fed, was shut in by a brick wall. This reared itself up along the passage that passed the kitchen windows, on its way to the back door. Eleanor's own sitting-room, upstairs at the back, where she sat and worked and received visitors, was shadowed on even the sunniest of days. Its main, lead-paned windows faced north, and there were many beautiful trees to be seen, dearly loved by Eleanor, but which again helped to shut out the light from that direction. The only other source of illumination was the skylight, through which the sun shone only obliquely, never directly. You could not count the two miniature porthole windows on either side of the fireplace. They were so minute and were generally obscured by various objects: a high-backed chair covered with a rug, a record-player and, during the Wimbledon season, a fat television set. This was lent to her by her niece, Joanie (Joan Jefferson-Farjeon) just for that fortnight. Eleanor would not have a television of her own but she was a Wimbledon enthusiast. It ran in her family—and so did cricket too.

It was strange, considering the closeness of our friendship, how many things Eleanor and I found we *didn't* have in common—cricket, tennis, crossword puzzles and alas, music.

It has always been a sorrow to me that I am not a real music lover. I am quite allergic to opera, except perhaps for some of the highly emotional melodic passages. Eleanor, of course, was steeped in music and a Wagnerite. Most of my friends were in tune with her, and they would be invited to spend the evening to listen with her, the telephone receiver being taken off, to an opera, a recital or a Promenade Concert.

I should record that, under Eleanor's wise and careful guidance, I did become more appreciative of better music, and I am not now as much of a Philistine in that sphere as I may have suggested.

One thing we did share was a love of antique furniture and bric-à-brac. She had spent a lot of money on such things before I met her. Eleanor knew good pieces when she saw them and had a child's delight in pretty things. But she had not the flair—or I must admit the space—for showing them off. Her house was filled to overflowing with lovely pieces of furniture and *objets d'art*, mostly wasted, because ill-displayed. She cared not at all for appearances in general and was not attracted by the thought of gracious living.

On the other hand no one enjoyed an outing more. Dinner at the Garrick Club for instance. I took her there one evening early on in our friendship and the *gourmet* in her did more than justice to the food and wine. When, after dinner, I returned from the pay-desk to our table I found Eleanor had been appropriated by another member, and was seated at his table enjoying a glass of old port and a cigar.

In those days I used to hear a great deal about her cigar-smoking. A friend of ours once described her as: 'A great, lovable, mischievous, warm-hearted, generous Bohemian, with cigar-smoking propensities.' This could have been a description of George Sand, but not of Eleanor Farjeon, as this friend realised when he got to know her better. But when people came who smoked and offered her a cigarette or occasionally a cigar, Eleanor would light up with the best of them. Alone with me, a non-smoker, I never once saw her light even a cigarette.

Her cigar-smoking with characters like Leon M. Lion, and her outbreak at the Garrick Club dinner were, I consider, all part of Eleanor's childlike love of being left out of nothing, of being *in* on everything, of playing the part that suited the company of the moment.

I have said it was not for nothing that she was half-Jewish. I would also add that it was not for nothing either that she was the granddaughter of the American actor Joseph Jefferson. I have always remembered one of her crises when Eleanor's nephew, Gervase Farjeon, had reason to say to me, "Poor Denys," to which I responded, "Poor Nellie." And to this he replied, "Oh, drama has always gone on round Nellie."

I was to become increasingly aware of the truth of that statement as, in the years that followed, I came to a fuller understanding of his aunt's kaleidoscopic character. This love of drama was something in Eleanor's make-up with which I never entirely came to terms. Times without number I was surprised into being thrown by her highly-coloured account of a situation, or the alarmist note in her voice on the telephone when she told me of some item of bad news given out over the radio.

48

On one such occasion this habit of Eleanor's of creating drama cost me a night's sleep and a considerable sum of money. At midnight on Boxing Day 1962, she rang me and cried, "Are you without *light*?" She had forgotten for the moment that since the war-time black-out and the fuel crisis of 1947 I had had an exaggerated dread of being plunged into darkness. As a matter of fact there had been no failure in our district, but Hampstead had had an electric breakdown for about half an hour. Eleanor went on to say that the roads were blocked with snow everywhere, and altogether painted a picture of what seemed to my over-active imagination like a nation-wide freeze-up and an imminent failure of power. I slept little that night and by 8.30 a.m. was out buying up all the candles, nightlights and matches I could lay hands on; not to mention an expensive oil stove. It turned out to be unnecessary. Eleanor's Cassandra-like forebodings of the night before proved to be unfounded. There was no crisis and the oil stove stands unused in my hall to this day.

Perhaps this episode throws light on my own eccentricities rather than on Eleanor's. But it does at least serve as an example of the element in her character to which her nephew had referred and to which I shall be returning, when he said, "Oh, drama has always gone on round Nellie."

CHAPTER SIX

SO FROM EARLY 1950 onwards, as Eleanor said, we were getting to know each other. This meant also getting to know each other's relations and friends. I began by degrees to meet the various members of the family: 'Big Joan' (Mrs. Herbert Farjeon), so-called by Eleanor, not on account of *avoirdupois*, but merely to distinguish her from 'Joanie' (Joan Jefferson-Farjeon), the décor artist and daughter of Eleanor's brother Joe, the novelist and playwright. Then there were Gervase, the Herbert Farjeons' son, and his actress wife, Violetta; Gervase's two sisters, Joscelyn, wife of Ernest Frank the singer, and Annabel, the ballet critic, married to Dr. Igor Anrep. I like them all and I think they saw at once that I had nothing but honourable intentions towards their aunt.

Eleanor on her side became devoted to my brother and sister-in-law, Alban and Renée; theatre people and Catholics like me, with whom my life has always been blessedly and inextricably interwoven. In addition, there were countless friends on both sides, some of whose names will crop up from time to time.

When I was again questioning Eleanor about the happenings of that first year, I asked her if it was in 1950 that I first went with her to see Walter de la Mare. "No," she said in her most positive manner, "I hadn't then begun to take you to see people." "No," I replied with equal firmness, "but I'd taken *you* to see Sir Laurence Olivier!"

And so I had. Amongst the many plays we saw that winter was Christopher Fry's *Venus Observed* at the St. James's, which we both enjoyed nearly as much as we had admired Fry's adaptation of *Ring Round the Moon*. After the play we went behind to see Olivier whom I had known since he was seventeen. The meeting of these two, the old friend and the new, was highly entertaining. Larry was charming, friendly and amused. Eleanor was the usual warm, ebullient personality that came to the fore on such occasions. She astonished Olivier by saying, "I haven't felt like this since I used to be taken behind to see Henry Irving." "Now, Miss Farjeon, you're going *too* far," was the reply. But she added that Olivier was one of the rare actors whose physical presence, like Irving's, created an electric shock as soon as he appeared on the stage.

Although chronologically it happened later, I think I should pair off my bringing together of Eleanor and Laurence Olivier with her taking me to see Walter de la Mare.

She had known him for many years and in common with all his old friends called him 'Jack'. Although by this time, at the age of fifty, I had got used to meeting celebrities, I could not but be impressed at the thought of visiting such a very distinguished man of letters in his own home. I was not disappointed. Walter de la Mare was, in fact, the only famous figure whom I have met face to face without loss of illusion. His whole setting: the beautiful house in a backwater of Twickenham, the antique furniture highly polished, the gleaming silver and the brass, the view from the side windows of a green and quiet park. And on one of the windows,

engraved with an ordinary pin (so de la Mare told me) by
Laurence Whistler, were the poet's own words:

"Look thy last on all things lovely . . ."

We had an old-fashioned, sit-down tea of delicious bread
and butter, and scones and cakes, home-made by his faithful
nurse-companion whom he called 'N'. At tea-time he
revealed a Puckish vein. He reminded me then a little of Lob
in Barrie's *Dear Brutus*. Especially when he looked at me suddenly and said, "Are you dull of comprehension?" Having
allowed sufficient pause for me to show discomfiture, he then
went on, "Sometimes I think *I'm* dull of comprehension
because . . ." But Walter de la Mare's manners were charming
and as a host he was a model of unaffected courtesy. Although
then over eighty he was a handsome, distinguished-looking
man.

Eleanor on this occasion was quite different from the
woman I had taken to see Olivier. Walter de la Mare was an
old and treasured friend and they talked naturally and
lovingly as old friends do. They spoke of other old friends,
and I sat spellbound as I heard the names being tossed into the
air: names I had seen as a schoolboy over thirty years ago in
the first anthology I had ever owned, *Poems of Today*, and in
a rather later collection of Methuen's: names such as Siegfried
Sassoon, Ralph Hodgson, Edward Thomas, James Stephens,
Lascelles Abercrombie. . . . No wonder my host said of me to
Eleanor that my silences were eloquent! She told me this as
a compliment, but it could have been taken either way
coming from that Lobish mind.

I remember one concrete thing he told me about the writing of poetry: that it was a great mistake to think that every line must be a poetic gem. He said we must have the more prosaic lines in between to act as a setting for the jewels.

He was getting tired and Eleanor knew it was time for us to go. Before we left she put into de la Mare's hands an autograph book, satin-bound and full of illustrious signatures. She had bought it in an antique shop and had given it to me. Walter de la Mare promised that when he felt strong enough he would write something in it for me and have it returned by post.

After a week or two the book arrived and he had granted me my special request. He had written in his own hand-writing the verse beginning, "Look thy last on all things lovely," the verse I had seen engraved by Whistler on the window-pane. But to my surprise and disappointment he had shared a page in the book with someone whose signature was indecipherable; his identity unknown. In writing to thank him I drew his attention to this modesty and assured him that I should cut out his verse and paste it as was fitting on to a page by itself to be shared by no other.

Almost by return he wrote begging me not to spoil my beautiful book. To prevent my doing so, he had taken the trouble to write out on a separate piece of paper a little poem, shortly to be published in a new volume, The Owl, which I could use instead.

CHAPTER SEVEN

"WE SHALL NEVER be done with talking, you and I", is the first line of a poem that I was one day to write to Eleanor. And how we did talk. Upstairs by the fire in the sitting-room, down in the kitchen where we had our meals and, in the summer, out in the garden under the copper beech's shade or in the Garden Room. All through that year of 1950 we talked and talked and talked. There was no subject barred to Eleanor Farjeon. She told me that her sister-in-law, 'Big Joan', once said, "Nellie's the only one of the family that has no inhibitions." She was right. There was nothing you could not discuss with her or ask her opinion about. In the right sense of the word she was unshockable. She was even capable of being Rabelaisian when the situation called for it.

In all that talking I was able to counteract some of the effects of my Philistine upbringing and catch up on my mis-spent youth—mis-spent in dreaming and intellectual laziness. I came, for instance, to understand and appreciate poetry in a way I had never done before.

But perhaps most important of all, I began to learn from Eleanor the long lessons of coming to terms with my temperament. I learned, at least in theory, from her wise counsels and her practical example, how to deal with the demands of my own clamorous nature. I saw the disastrous effects of my passionate possessiveness and megalomania. I realised fully for the first time the importance of sharing my friends with others, the ruin brought about by vengeful ragings and resentments, the scorings off, the hittings back, the writing of angry letters.

You just could not live close to Eleanor Farjeon without learning the theory of these things. I stress the theoretical aspect as I should not wish to suggest anything but the plain truth: that it was an uphill climb, with still far too little to show for it after all these years.

A few fragments from verses written later on will serve to show the direction in which Eleanor's philosophy and way of life were leading my uncertain steps:

> To love and let the loved one go,
> There true loving's secret lies;
> Holding love is loving's foe . . .

and

> Perfection's image, immutable and constant,
> Never in imperfect human kind
> Will you discover;
> A way of love more perfect you must find,
> The way to be of human frailties
> The perfect lover.

And in another poem these words:

> . . . to love,
> Each stranger that we meet, each friend,
> And never hate the hating one . . .

To strike a lighter note and quote a better poet, here is a four-lined verse, typical of Eleanor's wit, wisdom and technical deftness, written to me when she realised the acute sense of urgency by which I am driven.

> Learn to live leisurely, said Nellie Farjeon,
> Learn to live leisurely, do;
> You'll find that in Time there is always a margin,
> And the margin of Time is for you.

In later days Eleanor used to call me Mr. Playgent. This was my name for the other side of my character, in which the element of urgency was most plainly to be seen. Mr. Playgent could be as daring and determined as his counterpart was diffident and easily discouraged. Mr. Playgent was a planner, pursuing his small aims and ambitions with all the concentration of a Big Business man; looking always several moves ahead with the eye of a champion chess player.

As to Eleanor's verse the day was far off before I could even attempt to reply in that form or on that level. But here is one of the many letters written at this period which will reveal the relationship between us, and show that already I was keenly conscious of my great debt to her.

Undated

You've left the receiver off, I believe! I've been trying to get you for about an hour!

I'm like Simon's wife's mother, "sick of a fever"—in bed with a basin by my side. Only a chill I think. All will be well tomorrow.

I must write you a little letter to thank you for your long

one. Yes, I am knowing now a great deal of interior peace
—and am filled with gratitude.

You've played your part, dearest 'e', in this year of
healing. I shall never forget it.

It's early days; and as you say there is bound to be
suffering—but I, too, believe it will be different and that I
shall be better equipped to meet it . . .

I can't write more dear.

Thank you again most lovingly for everything . . .

P.S. Tomorrow (Friday) night I am doing a Third
Programme Broadcast—on Thomas Gray. 9–9.30 I believe.
But it's unexpected and I haven't seen the script. I may be
terrible!

I wasn't terrible; because I was not required to read romantic verse to which I have always considered my voice un-
suited. Some prose narration in the character of Sir Horace
Walpole fell to me, which was far more in my line. I was
able to tell Eleanor after the broadcast that I had on that
occasion for the first time met Dylan Thomas.

He had arrived at the end of the day to rehearse a long,
little-known poem of Gray's, which he spoke in heavy,
thunderous tones which seemed to me then displeasing and
lacking in variety. Perhaps even Dylan Thomas's voice was
more suited to one kind of verse than to another?

He struck me as almost plain and lacking in charm and
friendliness. Perhaps he was shy? I remember he wore the
loudest check-patterned shirt I have ever seen.

The opening sentences of my letter to Eleanor amuse me

now. Had she taken the receiver off? I wonder. She could, and did, leave it off from carelessness as we all do; or deliberately take it off because she wanted to listen undisturbed to an opera or a concert. But she could just as easily have been in the middle of one of her major sessions of telephoning to which I had not yet become acclimatised and about which I want to write a little later on.

CHAPTER EIGHT

'*The Silver Curlew* was revived the following Christmas. When its run was ended in 1951, I presented myself at Farm Street; and on 22nd August I was baptised in Spanish Place, a very old baby of 70. Denys Blakelock, twenty years younger, was my Godfather.'

This was Eleanor herself writing an autobiographical article, 'My Latter Years', in John Pudney's *The Book of Leisure* of 1957.

The Silver Curlew was revived that Christmas and Eleanor *was* received by Father Richard Mangan, S.J.

I should explain that this happened round about the time when Eleanor's popular poem, 'Mrs. Malone', had been published, and she had given Father Mangan a copy. Each verse ended with the words, ' "There's room for another," said Mrs. Malone.' And the last line of all, spoken at Heaven's Gate by St. Peter, runs, ' "There's room for another one, Mrs. Malone." '

The ceremony of Eleanor's christening and reception was performed in the baptistry at St. James's, Spanish Place. I was present as her sponsor, or godfather. I could not follow it closely as the ceremony was in Latin. Suddenly, to my amazement, I heard Father Mangan breaking into English and some very unexpected English words too. The ceremony was over and what Father Mangan said was, "There's room for another one, Mrs. Malone."

There was probably nobody of Eleanor's family or friends who did not at that time take it for granted that I was entirely responsible for her becoming a Catholic. This is what Eleanor herself had to say upon the subject in a letter with which she enclosed two poems:

March 25th 1954

Here they are, for you to keep if you like. The strange thing to me is that they were never commissioned, never printed, never copied, and not written (like the Carols and others) to fit some particular season or occasion—they were simply written, because, it seems, I felt I had to. The strange thing is that I seemed to be saying more than I knew, and that having said it I left it there till—or rather, it was left there till November 1949, when you became His instrument to hold out a hand to me. If anyone thought, or thinks, that I took to Religion *because* of you, these might convince them that I took to Religion because of God. I don't know though if they are good poems. You tell me.

The verses have no titles, are written in longhand and are both signed underneath in the same words.

> Lord, Thou Who gav'st me all I have,
> My mind's delight, my body's power,
> All that in coming to the grave
> I must let fall like summer's flower,
> One thing Thou didst to me accord
> I still shall keep: my need of Thee, O Lord.

Thou didst that everlasting gift
Upon my cradled sleep bestow
That I in life might never lift
My head, might nothing do or know
Which in itself could perfect be
Unless, O Lord, I turned my face to Thee.

No joy wherein Thou hast no part,
Nor love but Thou the soul of it,
Nor grief that shuts Thee from its heart,
Nor suffering that can Thee omit;
From these if Thou be absent, I
To heaven in my need of Thee must cry.

So even, from my coffined sleep
When I awake, the single thing
Which I among Thy gifts may keep
Shall carry me upon its wing
Into Thy presence, where Thy Word
At last shall fill my need of Thee, O Lord!

Eleanor Farjeon
(written many years ago and
rediscovered in March 1954.)

More lovely than the noonday rest
In summer heat
When the warm earth gives every guest
A welcome sweet.
Is that content by which I am possessed
When I am laid at my Creator's feet.

More wonderful than rest at night
When Heaven charms
Slumber with spells whose starry light
Allays alarms,
Is that repose which covers sense and sight
When I am held in my Creator's arms.

More perfect than the ease can be
When old ones rest,
Or they the sleep of infancy
Before life's test,
Is that last breath of peace which falls on me
When I am cast on my Creator's breast.

Eleanor Farjeon
(written many years ago and
rediscovered in March 1954.)

Eleanor pays me the compliment in her letter of asking me whether these are 'good' poems. I hesitate to give an opinion, but they seem to me to lack the special magic that one associates with her infallible poetic touch. I decided to include them, however, because of their exceptional interest as an indication of her spiritual development and her early instinctive turning towards a Creator, all the more remarkable in view of her lack of any kind of religious upbringing.

Her niece, Annabel Farjeon, spoke the plain truth when she said to a mutual friend, John McBennett, "Here we are, good God-fearing pagans—and Nellie becomes a Roman Catholic!"

It is important to include also another extract from the

article in *The Book of Leisure*, showing as it does that Eleanor Farjeon did not take this important step without a great deal of thought, and stressing that her conclusions had their beginnings in her philosophical reading of many years before.

'I found myself reading books that were new to me (though many of them were the oldest in the world), Saint Augustine, The Imitation of Christ, and Elected Silence; and the Gospels as I had never read them before. I asked myself questions I had not thought of asking; and having no faith from which to be converted, I simply found myself still further on a road I had been travelling from my first reading of Plato when I was a girl. I began to realise that the streaming spirit of love between man and God, of which I had become so certain as my years moved from maturity to old age, was the Holy Ghost.'

After Eleanor became a Catholic she went, over the first three years, to several Retreats given by Fr. Benignus C.P. (Congregation of the Passion) at the Cenacle Convent, Hampstead. She had met him through me and had taken a great liking to this exceptional priest, with his warm humanity and beguiling Irish tones.

During the last Retreat Eleanor made notes of his Conferences and sent them to me. Valuable though they are they would hardly be suitable for inclusion in this book. But there is one particular extract, dealing with a period between the Conferences, that is so delightfully descriptive of Eleanor Farjeon's simplicity and humour that I could not bring myself to withhold it from readers of this Memoir.

'I sat in the sunny garden under a tree before lunch, reading my Bible like a good girl, and Fr. Benignus walked by saying his rosary like a good boy. He stopped by me and said, "I'm keepin' me eye on you." I answered, "And I'm keeping my ear on you." "Ah, an' did ye like it now?" I told him how much I liked it now, then he talked about your motor car, and then he went on saying his rosary like a good boy, and I went on reading my Bible like a good girl.'

After she had been received Eleanor showed the childlike side of her character in her naïve attitude towards Confession. "I never can think of anything to confess," she would say to everyone. (I used secretly to call this her Little Jack Horner rôle.)

It is quite true that Eleanor must have had very little to confess and only venial sins at that. I should not imagine she committed a single mortal sin after she became a Catholic. But, truly good and selfless as she was, even Eleanor was not impeccable, impregnable. After all, we are told that the smallest imperfection is of the nature of sin. I would have thought there might have been tiny imperfections with which she could have made 'matter' for Confession, as the theologians put it.

It was ingenuous and amusing, of course. But it used slightly to worry me, her over-scrupulous, Calvinistic godfather. I have always had a healthy fear of an intensely personal Devil, and feel he lies in wait for those of us who are over-confident of our spiritual unassailability.

I must say that in the last years of her life you never heard Eleanor mention this difficulty about Confession. On the contrary, she quite often found fault with herself for complaining or for having given in to self-pity. From the onlooker's point-of-view this reproach was unnecessary, for Eleanor was a great sufferer from many small discomforts. The generalised fibrositis alone must have been hard to bear; and she could never even know the relief of soaking in a hot bath, owing to the dangers of unsteadiness, and of muscular inflexibility; not to mention the lack of a bathroom—or even hot water—upstairs, in that strange, antiquated house of hers. In all this she was as ever an example to me of patient endurance and unselfishness.

But how difficult it is to give a true account of another human being's personality and character. Despite anything I have said in this chapter, I must stress the fact that Eleanor for the most part was humble and contrite. She certainly had humility about her work, although she once surprisingly said to me, "You're vain and I'm conceited." But I think, as one of her relatives said to me, if she was conceited it was more about the Family of Farjeon than about herself. Towards her own work she had no false modesty, but she was far too detached and severely self-critical to be conceited about it.

CHAPTER NINE

EARLIER IN THE summer of that year, Eleanor and I went on what I always called our 'honeymoon' holiday. It was a fortnight in June which we spent in Cornwall. A week at Looe and a week at Marazion. It was very successful.

There is nothing like a holiday to reveal a friend's foibles and funny little ways. Eleanor discovered several of mine, I am sure; and I uncovered many of hers.

There was the affair of the Single Egg, for instance. At Marazion we ordered fried eggs and bacon. They brought me bacon and two eggs. Eleanor was given bacon and one egg.

"Why two eggs for Mr. Blakelock and only one for me?" she asked. "A gentleman's portion, Madam," the waitress replied. But Eleanor would not accept this inequality of the sexes, and before many moments had passed she was tackling her second egg with enthusiasm.

The episode of the Single Egg, however, was responsible for producing the first of the many verses with which Eleanor decorated our days in Cornwall to my great delight.

Life

Boiled eggs for breakfast! Hearts begin to throb!
The Cock does the crowing, the Hen does the job.
Boiled eggs for breakfast! *Isn't that like men!*
Two for the Cock, and one for the Hen!

June 1st, 1951

This was my first—no, my second—insight into an un-expected side of Eleanor's character. The first occasion on which it was brought to my notice was when, in the Spring of the same year, I had taken her one day for a surprise picnic. The destination was the surprise. I drove her for some miles without telling her where she was being taken to. At last I stopped outside an old country church in a secluded spot.

"Where are you?" I asked her.

"Haven't the faintest idea," she said.

Eleanor had no bump of locality anyway, (partly, perhaps, on account of her bad sight).

"Look at the clock on the church tower," I said.

No, that didn't give her a clue. The church clock did *not* still stand at ten to three. So how could she know it was Grantchester?

Soon we unpacked our picnic lunch—cheeses, I think, and Guinness. A half pint bottle each. I opened one and divided it between the two of us, as I like to keep Guinness with a head on it to the end. Then I broached the second bottle, and poured it, I must admit, in rather unequal shares into our respective glasses.

"Here!" cried Eleanor, "I don't call that at all fair. Those are not equal. You've got far more than I have."

This episode caused a lot of good-natured laughter. But all the same it showed me for the first time an important feature of Eleanor's character. 'Fair's fair' was her attitude towards everything, and scrupulously fair. And it came, I think, from two sources.

Firstly, her brother Harry's training. He ruled that nursery

67

in the Nineties, and his was the sort of microscopically honest mentality that would make him pay a twopenny fare on one bus, if for some reason he'd been prevented from paying it on a previous one. Eleanor was Harry-trained, and just as honourable and honest. She would never for instance have dreamed of cheating the Income Tax of a penny.

There is a second element that plays a part in this attitude towards finance: her Jewish blood. Like all Jewish people she was generous to a fault (she gave away hundreds of pounds), but she could not bear to be done down by a halfpenny, unless she herself made a point of cancelling a debt, which she often did.

Eleanor was extremely good at finance and, like most of us, loved getting something cheap or driving a bargain. Because of this, almost the only thing that was inclined to irritate her was bad shopping, and a failure to keep an account of the money spent. The women and girls who worked for Eleanor adored her, and she was most generous and concerned for their welfare. But one of them did say to me once, "Miss Farjeon gets quite cross." And it was always because the girl had taken the first thing that was given her and had brought back something inferior, making a muddle of the actual cost.

Her standards about shopping and the quality of foods linked up largely with the fact that she had revelled in marketing as long as she was well enough to do it for herself. She loved the colours of the flowers and fruit and vegetables, the press of people, and finding the best of everything for the best prices.

But I have wandered far from the 'honeymoon'. In Looe

she became in many ways Little Nellie on a summer holiday again, enjoying every minute of the sea, hunting excitedly round the local shops for 'holiday presents' for me and to take back home to others. She liked, too, the ease of hotel life and the good meals.

Eleanor told me early on she was a *gourmet,* and confessed to me that she had also been a *gourmande.* Perhaps she had been. I know that when she turned her mind seriously to spiritual matters she looked upon this as one of the weaknesses she had to watch. She certainly ate very little towards the end of her life but continued to cater generously for me.

Then there was the question of clothes in Cornwall. I came eventually completely to accept the fact that Eleanor had little sense of dress, or of the fitness of things in that field. She would, for instance, wear the most unsuitable frocks and coats for theatre-going occasions. What is more, she had the courage not to care. As long as she was comfortable that was all that mattered.

But I was more conventionally minded than she was and very self-conscious. I was therefore rather taken aback on our first night at Looe to see her striding into the dining-room in plimsolls. There were few, if any, in evening dress, but all the women put on something special for dinner; and there was a general air of smartness and a handsome head-waiter whom Eleanor had rather a fancy for. Again she wore plimsolls when I drove her over to Fowey one Sunday evening to see the du Mauriers. We had quite a battle about those plimsolls.

I need not have worried. I had expected to find the old

order that one had associated with the du Mauriers at Cannon Hall, Hampstead—tennis and smart people from London. But when we arrived and rang the bell, the door was slowly opened by Jeanne du Maurier, who spoke to us in a whisper, the whisper of the sick room; and as she spoke I saw, far away in the background, Lady du Maurier moving silently out of sight. Jeanne apologised for not inviting us in, but told us her mother was very ill indeed and saw no one. It was a sad visit, like an episode from one of Daphne du Maurier's own novels. I thought of Lady du Maurier in the old days, so friendly and charming. We drove away, through the dark, wet Sunday evening back to Looe. The next morning we left prematurely and went on to Marazion.

How little those plimsolls had mattered. And Eleanor always suffered from foot trouble. They were comfortable. But I had not then learned to stop trying to 'improve' people, to mould them to the image I thought they ought to be.

This passion for improvement was exercised a great deal on poor Eleanor. I persuaded her, for instance, to have writing-paper printed with a proper letter-heading. "You've given me dignity," she said. But her hair-do was a problem. The hair itself was exceptionally fine and soft. And then, her sight was so bad that she just could not see to do it properly. Once and once only I got her to a hairdresser. That was when the Queen Mother was to attend an R.A.D.A. performance of *The Silver Curlew*. She wisely had her hair done the afternoon before, and on the day itself, when the formal waves had begun to loosen, Eleanor looked charming. But she was incorrigible.

She refused ever again to 'waste time and money' having her hair regularly or even occasionally done. And when, on the night of the Royal Performance, she sat at supper on the stage alone with the Queen Mother, believe it, or believe it not, *she wore no gloves*.

★

At some kind of gathering to which literary 'fans' are lured, that they may have the chance of meeting their favourite writers, Eleanor was present.

She told me that an ill-mannered 'fan'—a woman—came up to her, saw the name 'Eleanor Farjeon' on the label pinned to her dress, looked into her face and said, "Good Heavens! I always thought of you as red-headed and frightfully pixie."

The matter of personal appearance played a bigger part in Eleanor's life and make-up than was plain either to herself or to the ordinary beholder. She was violently allergic to any kind of publicity and was reluctant to allow photographs to appear. When she won the Carnegie Medal for *The Little Bookroom*, and later the first Hans Andersen Medal and America's Regina Medal, she was as tremendously pleased and excited as only Eleanor could be. But at the approach of a daily paper for an interview and a photograph, she got into an emotional state, went to bed and had the reporters turned away.

On the other hand she was inconsistent in this matter. Anything distinguished, such as an article in the *Times Literary Supplement*, or appreciations in *The Horn Book of America*, she was human enough to welcome with delight. There was a protective screen to hide behind with the serious articles, whereas the other represented that probing into her private life and personality that she disliked above all things.

But whatever Eleanor may have felt about the question of looks, she cannot with maturity have failed to realise that her Creator had more than made up to her for the lack of physical beauty.

The last sequence in *The Silver Curlew* is the christening of the Royal Infant. This whole enchanting scene, enhanced by Clifton Parker's original and melodious music, always reminded me of the Nativity. (I little knew that Eleanor's own christening was to take place a year and a half later.)

King Nollekens and Queen Doll with the baby in her arms sat there with the Court gathered round in joyful adulation. On to the scene, announced one by one, came the Fairy Godmothers each bearing a casket:

The Morning Fairy, with the gift of a Kind Heart.

The Noontide Fairy, with a gift of Happiness.

The Twilight Fairy, with a gift of Beauty.

The Midnight Fairy, with the gift of Magic.

Although Eleanor Farjeon had no christening in her infancy, all these Fairies she wrote about so charmingly must indeed have been present at her birth.

The gift of a Kind Heart? Anyone who met Eleanor for five minutes could not but have felt her charity, her compassion and her gentleness.

The gift of Happiness? Could anything depress for long the enthusiasm, the zest for life, the spirit of innocent joy that belonged so especially to Eleanor?

The gift of Magic? Did she not enchant the minds of countless children with her magical touch in poetry and prose, her singing games, her Nursery Rhymes of London Town?

And the gift of Beauty? Well, that is a relative quality anyway; and if conventional 'looks' were denied to Eleanor, the beauty of her spirit shone through and showed itself in the sweetness and mildness of her habitual expression and in the deep, grave look of true concern she gave to anyone who came to lay their troubles bare to her and to seek her sympathy and her wise advice.

CHAPTER TEN

ALTHOUGH THE CORNISH holiday was so successful it was during those two weeks away from home that Eleanor first saw my phobia in operation, and that I discovered she had a phobia of her own.

At Looe we had two small narrow rooms next to each other with a delightful view looking straight down on to the sea. Every afternoon we had a siesta before going out for a drive. One day when tea time came, I found, on trying to open my bedroom door, that either the key had been turned from outside or—worse still—the mechanism had broken down. I couldn't open it. I was locked in.

Fortunately for me, Eleanor was still in her room and heard my cries for help. For some reason the door opened at once for her and I was rescued. But Eleanor never forgot the sight of me gasping for breath, with my coat flung off, my collar undone, my shirt torn open. She knew then how very real this problem was.

On the other hand, one day when we were exploring a Cornish village by the sea, I found that Eleanor was abnormally afraid of heights. I could not induce her to come up on to the cliffs, even at a spot a hundred yards away from the precipitous edge. Only in March 1965, while I was in process of finishing this book, I rang her one evening and heard her say emphatically, "Thank God". "Why, particularly?" I asked. "A man has just walked out into space," was the reply. It was the Russian astronaut having his first swim in the sky. Eleanor had heard of it over the radio and the very thought of it had set her imagination working.

During our time in Cornwall Eleanor kept me almost daily supplied with *vers de l'occasion*. A visit to the Lizard and a disappointing lunch produced this:

Lunch at the Lizard

(Triolet)
"Let's lunch at the Lizard
On lobsters and cream!
Come tempest, come blizzard,
We'll lunch at the Lizard.
Oh, *won't* that be wizard!"—
'Twas just a bad dream,
Our lunch at the Lizard
Sans lobster and cream.

1.6.'51

An admittance from me of a personal vanity, what we called my 'uppitty' quiff of hair, brought this to the collection:

When your hair is uppitty
You are just my cup o' tea!
But you are not my drop o' tea
When your hair is floppity!

5.6.'51

A poem in the Housman manner was written on the

75

occasion of my having to call at an oculist's at Redruth to have an ingrowing eyelash removed.

Song from "The Cornwall Lad"

Do you recall the eyelash, lad,
That streaked your young man's sight,
When sun shone grand on sea and sand
And drowned the world in light
        And beauty was All Right?

Oh joy of youth's all eyewash, lad!
Too soon we fail to cash
The golden glee of sand and sea
When life applies the lash,
        And beauty goes to smash.
           30.5.'51

Eleanor also introduced me for the first time to some lines which she had once composed for Pod straight off the cuff with her extraordinary facility.

Pod hated going off to school, more like a school*boy* than a master, and this had been an occasion when he was more unwilling than usual. Here is her own account of the incident and a copy of the old 'rune', as she called it, written out especially for me when I asked her permission to use it in print.

'You have my permission to use . . . The Impromptu Rune I recited over Pod's head one morning when he buried himself in the bedclothes instead of getting up to go to school. I pulled him up by the front of his pyjamas, but

76

when I let go he flopped back again. I enclose a copy in the vernacular.'

Ancient Rune in the Vernacular
to assist the Early Rising of Reluctant Yokels

Now zitty oop, my vitty lad,
An' zitty oop, Oi zay,
Vor thou must dree the Barley-weird
Avoör the bröake o'day.

Then down ee vlopped, the vitty lad,
Azackerly as Oi veared—
"Oi will not roise at bröake o'day
To dree the Barley-weird."

An impromptu by Eleanor Farjeon
on a Necessary Occasion.
It was completely ineffective.

I used often in later times to get her to say The Vitty Lad for me. This absurdity never failed to make me laugh coming from Eleanor in that exaggerated, bogus country dialect known to actors as 'Mummerset.' And yet it had an authentic ring about it too, as if in fact it could have been unearthed from some old book of folk rhymes.

Eleanor's knowledge of poetry and her ear for verse of any period fooled the experts on one occasion. In The Shepheard's Gyrland from Faithful Jenny Dove she invented an Elizabethan poet, Nathaniel Downes, and wrote several poems as if composed by him. So brilliantly were they done, and so completely in the manner of the period, that she took in some of the literary scholars. She had a serious enquiry as to whether he was a genuine poet whom she had discovered. She had made him seem so authentic that they really believed he might have existed and been overlooked.

Eleanor confessed the truth to them of course. She told me that when, many years later, she showed the poems of 'Natty' Downes to Edward Thomas he had said he would have guessed they were not genuine, because of the particular form she had used in the last poem of all.

An example of her gift for writing good poetry or clever lyrics quickly was 'The Night Will Never Stay'. This is one of her most popular and charming poems, and is to be found in countless anthologies. It was written on the stairs at a Hampstead party, while she was waiting outside during a guessing game.

It was not for nothing that Eleanor wrote a poem, under the pseudonym of Tom Fool, for five days of every week for ten years, in the *Daily Herald*. This must have greatly increased her natural facility; and accounts for the brilliant ease of her comic verses when she collaborated with her brother Bertie in works such as *Kings and Queens* in later times.

Eleanor often spoke to me of things like this out of the past, things that threw light on her industrious employment of her great and various talents.

She told me of a short story competition she went in for in her teens. Hers did not win the prize, but her father's words to her after he had read it meant far more to Eleanor than any award. When late in life she produced a successful book, like *The Little Bookroom*, or won three medals in a row, I used to repeat those words of her father's to her: "I have hopes of you, Nell." How proud he would have been had he lived to see her awarded the Carnegie medal and the Hans Andersen medal, both for *The Little Bookroom*. Also America's Regina medal, a recognition of her life's work for children. The Carnegie is for the best children's book of the year, the Hans Andersen for 'continued distinguished contribution to children's literature.' Eleanor was the first writer to receive the Hans Andersen, and her book was chosen from a selection of children's books from fifteen competing countries.

To return to Pod for a moment. There were many of his sayings which Eleanor told me of, and which I often used to quote to her delight.

"By God, Nell—you *do* wear well!" This expression of an undeniable truth I took over. Eleanor was indeed a stimulating companion. The years could not dim her originality of outlook, nor custom stale the freshness and unexpectedness of her fertile mind.

Then there was Pod's remark as he and Eleanor came out of a very inferior film to which they had gone on chance one day to pass the time: "Upon my soul, Nell, we'd have been better employed in downright iniquity."

As an example of Eleanor's sense of fun and of the ridiculous: there was an occasion when I drove her up to Oxford in the summer of 1950, to visit James Roose Evans, now well-known in the theatre, whom I had introduced to Eleanor. He was then a student at St. Benet's Hall, where they gave me hospitality for the night. Eleanor stayed at the Mitre. I left her there when we arrived, so that she could spend some time alone in Oxford, which was redolent with memories of previous visits with Pod.

That night we saw a beautiful production of *A Midsummer Night's Dream* in New College Garden. The following morning we met Jimmie Roose Evans and were introduced to the Company at the Playhouse and drank coffee in the bar. On our way out, preparatory to starting off for London, a quarrel began between Jimmie and me. Eleanor, as I have said, had little sense of dress or of what suited her, though she could be obstinate on the subject if you tried to interfere. On this particular trip she was wearing the most unbecoming hat I ever saw on the head of woman, and I chose this moment to beg her, on such a mild summer day, to take it off. Jimmie disagreed, which infuriated me, and our voices began to rise in a manner most unbecoming to Oxford's dignified surroundings. As we turned the corner into St. Giles, Eleanor seized the offending hat from off her head and thrust it through a grating into the basement quarters of a stranger's house, from which it was irretrievable. This gay, abandoned gesture brought the fighting to a close. I have often wondered what happened to that hat. Could it ever have adorned the head of another woman? I think not. I hope not, anyway.

CHAPTER ELEVEN

THIS CHAPTER IS mainly concerned with what I think of as The Newcastle Story: an adventure which could have been a misadventure and one in which Eleanor Farjeon will be seen playing the dual rôle of Dick Turpin and the Scarlet Pimpernel.

★

The Cornish holiday had been done in 'Fixer', the name given to Eleanor's Hillman Minx whose registration number was FXR 123. But soon after our return, having tasted for the first time since the War the freedom of motoring, which solved some of my problems of getting about, I bought a Bond Minicar, a minute motor with a two-stroke engine, which had only recently been put on the market. I chose this because it was cheap to buy, cheap to run, cheap and easy to garage at my flats. It was a small car, but it was to play a big part in our lives in the coming months.

In August I was offered a short but extremely rewarding part in *The White Sheep of the Family* with Jack Hulbert, and before we opened in London with it we had to do a provincial tour. So early in September I found myself facing the hazards of the road, heading for Liverpool, in this inadequate and alarming form of transport. No one would accompany me on the first long journey. I took thirteen hours, going twenty-five miles out of my way to avoid what were for me the terrors of the Mersey Tunnel.

The next morning, with the Dress Rehearsal in front of me, I could only scribble a letter-card to Eleanor.

Liverpool

Here I am. No major mishaps, but it took me 13 hours. The last lap was pretty grim—so much traffic and the sun in my eyes a lot of the time. I don't think Minnie will do for long journeys—but that's for the future. After supper, I put the car away and went to Confession at the pro-Cathedral just opposite, so I didn't do badly. Then I unpacked and went to bed—and to sleep immediately from 11 to 5.15! Have just been to 10 o'clock Mass. Thought much of you. Darling Eleanor, you are *wonderful*. What will you think of next? I didn't count them, but there appeared to be about 6 dozen roses, red and pink. Simply lovely—and the card too. Thank you for it all, my dearest. You are known here both for your books and The Curlew, so you've started me off well.

God bless you, and have a real rest.

And on the Tuesday morning, after the First Night:

Tuesday

What a lot of things I have to thank you for—One thing after another—letters, telegrams, and the wonderful First Night parcel. How I love the Our Father [a tiny medallion]. I'm 'wearing' it in my waistcoat pocket on the stage. Lavender, handkerchiefs and on and on you go. Angus [Macleod] spoke so warmly about you last night, and said what a *good* person you were. A lot from him. So you are. And God will be glad you are 'greedy'—the Lord loveth a greedy pray-er? And how your prayers have been answered for me. I'm through it all. Even the terrible electric light failure from 6.15 to 7.45. The whole of Liverpool. I can't write more now; but the cuttings will tell you things you want to know . . .

The week at Liverpool passed as uneventfully as any week in any theatre ever does; and on the following fateful Sunday I set out over the Pennines for Newcastle. I started tired, but at least this time I had a reliable friend and companion with me, Derek Blomfield.

I seem alas! to have no letters from Eleanor written at this time, though there was always one waiting for me at every port. Once again mine to her must be the mirror in which the part she played can be seen, and they will show the way events were heading.

Newcastle-on-Tyne
Monday

How good you are to me. There's so much to thank you for—all the letters that see me in, and see me out—at each large, noisy city. It does make such a difference. Your letter and the wonderful cake—scrumptious indeed—plus dear Mrs. Gaynor's lights and roaring fire made quite a homecoming last night, after another rather alarming day.

The traffic was terrible in the morning and at lunch-time I'd made up my mind to wire you to try to send Fixer with one of your part-time drivers, who would take poor Minnie away. She's little more capable of doing these long drives than her owner. We took $11\frac{1}{2}$ hours: and when I'm working all the week I'm just desperately tired, Eleanor darling. But I've only got two more journeys of any length, and this morning I feel the Fixer project would only bring fresh anxieties of its own, and be more worry than help.

Next week we hope to start at 8 and get it over before dark. The windscreen difficulty made the last hour or more really hazardous; I could hardly see for the dazzle. It's a great weakness with Minicars.

I wore your St. Christopher. I love it on the pin, as there is nowhere to put it on the car itself. I send you a little medal I found at Liverpool—a poor little thing meant for a child. Well, little Nellie shall have it from her god-father in memory of that morning—how long ago? Oh Eleanor, pray for me that I can take this particular cross and get by to the end.

Hardly had I posted that letter before I knew I could not go on. My nerve was failing me. The thought of the long weeks stretching ahead with the journey each Sunday in the Minicar filled me with dismay. In desperation I telephoned to Eleanor to ask if she could come to my rescue by lending me the Hillman which was little used; or by arranging for some car, any car, to be sent down. If she could, there was an actor in the company, John Paul, who could drive me. "Leave it to me," she cried. I rang off and returned to my rooms to await the results.

An hour later I had a wire (Eleanor loved telegrams):

ELEANOR

ARRIVING FRIDAY COMING BY NIGHT WITH HANDSOME GIANT
DRIVER

That evening I posted her this letter:

Newcastle

You are a marvel! And oh! how grateful I am to you for
it all. I am distressed that you should put off your
Greatham friends [the Meynells] at so late an hour for me.
But I know you know your friends best, and how to treat
them . . .

. . . It was just plain over-strain and fatigue through
attempting the almost impossible. It's thoughtful of you
to suggest Manchester too; but I feel the need is not suffi-
ciently urgent to warrant that; and that it would not be
good in many ways. But it will be wonderful to see you
on Friday and Saturday. I've got you bed and breakfast
just down the road for Friday and Saturday nights. Tea
and supper here Friday; lunch out with me before Saturday matinée; tea and supper here Saturday. (No bedroom
here for you.) I don't think you can get here by tea-time;
but we'll hope to see you. If you arrive after I've left, go to
Mrs. Threlfall and get a key and leave your things. Get
your Adonis to garage car at Dex Garage and bring ticket
to me at theatre.

Seats Will you let me know if it's safe to book a seat for
Friday night? Will you be up to it? And it seems very
unlikely you'll get here by 7. I don't *much* want you to
see it at a matinée first but I will book one for Sat. night
for certain.

85

Food Landladies find food a problem. So could you bring a little tea, butter, sugar, etc. and if you could bring a tin or two from that cupboard of yours, it would be a great help. And perhaps an egg or two from the bin? I only mention these because you will have so much to think of.

Don't forget the Certificate of Insurance for Fixer. I'm very glad it's not being left till Saturday morning. The performance would have made everything so rushed.

Eleanor and her handsome giant left Hampstead at 2.0 a.m. They drove through the night, picnicking on the way, got ahead of the rush hour at Doncaster, and were in Newcastle by 11 0 a.m.

Eleanor enjoyed every minute of this nocturnal adventure. She stayed for the rest of the week with me, and the handsome giant took the Minicar back to London. As he drove into his garage in Hampstead the steering wheel came away in his hands. So Eleanor Farjeon and her handsome giant had probably saved not only my reason but my life.

For the next two days after her dramatic arrival in Newcastle, Eleanor became to the *White Sheep* cast what Miss Trant was to the theatrical company in Priestley's *The Good Companions*. But on the Sunday morning we had to say goodbye again. She stood smilingly at the front door of the Newcastle 'digs' to see us off in Fixer; the stalwart John Paul in the driver's seat, Derek Blomfield by his side as the navigator, and myself sitting complacently in the back.

How different from the previous Sunday, thanks to Eleanor's organisation and unselfishness. I was soon *en route* for Manchester in comfort with the anxieties smoothed away, while she was travelling by train back to London and home.

CHAPTER TWELVE

THE REMAINDER OF the tour was successfully negotiated and we opened at the Piccadilly Theatre where we ran for a long time. Eleanor came there to my dressing-room a great deal as I had many 'waits' throughout the performance. The week-ends were spent with her up at Hampstead and we telephoned to each other every night.

This should have been a pleasant, peaceful period; but judging from the letters written by Eleanor that autumn, it would appear that in amongst the seemingly happy days there were as ever the urgencies and anxieties, the perplexities of human relationships, the depressions and the dark feelings of an almost cosmic enclosure. In fairness to myself mine was seldom the only drama that went on 'round Nellie', as Gervase put it, or under Nellie's roof.

Anyway, these letters of Eleanor's were written within forty-eight hours of each other, so she must have felt the need was great.

Oct. 31st 1951

I wish, my darling, you could be once in that strange region we call the Heart, and see yourself there, as you are in me. You have said more than once "you know the worst of me"—you'd see that there, and the best of you too, a best you mightn't recognise; and both so cherished and surrounded in love that they are inseparably one man. And yet, it isn't the *worst* or the *best* of you I love with a completeness I feel for no other living being. I love many, warmly and deeply, all of whom have a worst and a best, as you and I have. But that final completeness of love is perhaps, after all, something we can only feel for one person at a time; in this finite state we live in we can't help loving some people more and some less, and all I know is that I love you *most*, not your best or your worst, but you. Only God knows whom I mean by that; and in this life which seems to me to be becoming one of perpetual prayer, there is hardly a moment in which Eleanor Mary* is not beseeching for Denys Peter* peace of mind, joy of heart, and above all strength of will—so that you may never lose what you have helped me to gain. God bless you, my beloved—

And two days later:

All Souls Day 1951

I won't forget your "I love you most—I do" last night. Will you believe that I love you so profoundly that I could pray for you to love, still more, somebody who could give you more than I can: not more love, that seems so impossible, but with it the life we all feel in so much need of, humanly, to grow and be happy on. But even that wouldn't mean all steady happiness—that can *never* come from one other human being. And while we are human beings, it is most difficult to make it come steadily from

* Our respective Catholic baptismal names.

God. So the fluctuations of our own moods have per-
petually to be dealt with. But I believe I dare promise you
this, that as long as I live there is no moment when you
cannot count on, and turn to, the strength and constancy
of my heart—and after I have lived, still more. No mood
of yours, no silence or absence can change it. I love you in
and through God, and also in and for your beloved self.

Unfortunately I cannot find any response from me to these
wonderful letters. In their place I would like to print a
fragment, and another whole letter, which might just as well
have been written by me at this time:

"... Thank you for your reassurances. The security you
give me is precious beyond words ..."
In this next letter I called her 'Nellie' for the first time.

Yes—I've never before felt an urge to call anyone by a
name other than the one I knew them by first. But somehow, sometimes at least, I shall like to call you by your own
childhood name—the name you were called by in your
nursery in the '90s, by your Mother and all the brothers
you loved so dearly. Perhaps because you have honoured
me by saying more than once that you think of me a little
in the same sort of way as your brothers; and also because
I do feel very much part of your whole life, and not just
the bit of it since December 1949...
I loved your letter, dearest Eleanor, and it was so like
you to think of such a thing—to speak to me, in advance as
it were, from the other world. So I shall keep your letter

always and read it and take comfort, if and when that contingency comes about.

But I'm not going to anticipate such things. I'm selfish enough to wish that I could go first, for I should be most dreadfully sad without you now, dear Eleanor. And I feel I can't bear any more sadness, now that I've known—through you—such joy in loving.

But that's the weak 'me', I know. God, no doubt, has many more sorrows waiting for me, as a necessary part of my purgation and development. And whatever He sends, or permits, to happen, I know He'll give me the strength to meet.

But don't go yet—please. For, all joking apart, I don't, oh! I don't want to lose you, Nellie. But thank you for writing, dearest, and thank you for loving. And thank you for bearing with all my deformed thoughts and feelings and for confounding them with your own generous ways.

"I don't want to lose you, Nellie." It referred back to a true story I had told Eleanor of a humourless North country man I knew. He stood at the foot of his wife's bed when she was feeling extremely ill with a high temperature. Looking down at her he said in flat, lugubrious tones, "I don't want to lose you, Annie."

However, all emotional problems were soon to be crowded out by the thoughts of Christmas, my first to be spent up at Eleanor's. In 1949 we had not been on those terms and in 1950 I had been in the revival of *The Silver Curlew*, and Eleanor, who was staying with the Parkers, Yoma and Clifton, in St. John's Wood, had come to my flat for dinner and presents.

But by this Christmas our friendship had become consolidated and it had been taken for granted that I should go up to her place. (It seems natural to say 'her place'. Eleanor always called it '*ma* place', just as she called her niece 'ma Joanie', with her own individual way of saying the possessive pronoun.)

It was from Eleanor that I first learned the phrase 'making a Christmas' for someone. She made one for me that year of 1951 and every year from then onwards. Later my brother and his wife, Alban and Renée, used to join us for dinner and more presents.

I shall never forget my first sight of Eleanor's house at Christmastime. Nothing was too much trouble for her. Scarlet ribbons on the door-knocker, mistletoe in the hall; just inside the front room a crib with miniature Christmas trees in the foreground. For the rest, dotted about were Father Christmasses of all kinds, figures of fairies and strange little animals, witch-balls and snow and glistening tinsel. Upstairs, in her sitting-room, decorations everywhere. And oh! the presents. Parcel after parcel, all beautifully done up in gaily-coloured papers of the season and labelled with something special written for everyone.

For me there were the main presents, called just the 'mains', and then dozens and dozens of 'little extras', each thought out with loving care in relation to one's every need. I, on my part, responded with 'mains' and 'little extras' for her.

All the old Dickensian family Christmasses, which her generous, expansive, Jewish father had made for them, were being joyously repeated now in Nellie. And birthdays were the same.

When we re-met two years before at the Arts Theatre I had become rather cynical about such occasions. But Eleanor altered all that; she gave me back the Christmas I had lost, and made my birthday, too, something to look forward to with childlike pleasure once again.

I found among the letters something I wrote to her upon this subject:

. . . How I do thank you for giving me back the childlike joy in Christmas. How strange it all is. We spend our lives, in the light of modern psychology, trying to grow up. And when we've done that—then only can we go back and be childlike again—'Except ye become as a little child . . .' . . .

This attitude towards innocent festivity of every kind was carried on into other people's lives and homes. I think Eleanor received three or four hundred Christmas cards from all over the world; and posted presents to every member of her adored family, and to countless others who might feel lonely and forgotten.

The fact is that Eleanor Farjeon was a born Fairy God-mother. She could appear at any moment from out of the fireplace and say, "You *shall* go to the Ball." And you did.

These Christmasses of Eleanor's had their source, as I have said, in the far-off Victorian days, when Nellie the child was bewitched by the presents and stockings and Christmas trees and parties that were showered upon her by devoted parents and their many friends.

Nellie's childhood, apart from the painful shyness that she speaks of in *A Nursery in the Nineties,* was a radiantly happy one; so that she suffered not at all in adult life from that sense of living in a minor key experienced so often by those whose young days have been overshadowed by the unthinking cruelties and quarrellings of parents, who neither understood how to bring up children, nor how to navigate their unsuccessful marriages.

This unclouded childhood was surely responsible for Eleanor's sunny nature, for her confidence in life and in the goodness of her fellow human beings. I hardly ever knew her low-spirited until her very last years. In fact, I frequently remarked, with envy I am afraid, on her great capacity for enjoyment on the one hand and, yet, on the other her immunity from any serious sense of disappointment. I envied her indifference to the constantly changing temperatures of heat and cold, or to the sudden clouding over of a day that had been so bright before. I wished I had her vitality and imperviousness to the hunger that exhausted nerves can bring. Eleanor seemed to have everything both ways.

"It isn't *fair,* is it?" she would say to me, a triumphant but kindly twinkle in her eye.

CHAPTER THIRTEEN

THERE ARE TWO things I have not yet written about in detail in connection with Eleanor Farjeon: telephones and cats.

She was inseparable from both to anyone who knew her at all well. What a telephonist she was! So often, describing meetings with friends, she would say, "We had lots of lovely talk." For this purpose she would also use the telephone, thinking nothing of having an hour's conversation with one niece in particular.

On the other hand, as I have already mentioned, Eleanor was quite ruthless in removing the receiver if the telephone was likely to interrupt anything she wanted to listen to. And—favoured child of fortune that she was—she never seemed to be caught and rebuked by the Exchange as most of us are.

I myself think the telephone exists for two purposes only—business and love. Otherwise I look upon it as a disagreeable necessity, though one which I should hate to be without.

Eleanor took some time before she came to realise this, and when first we knew each other we went full steam ahead. At all times during the day, but particularly last thing at night. One evening fairly late, I was feeling exhausted but rang her just the same.

"Are you in bed?" I said.

"Yes!" she cried complacently, triumphant among the pillows.

"Lucky brute!" I said.

From that time on when she rang me she would start the conversation with, "Are you a lucky 'bwoot'?" (Eleanor could not pronounce her r's and was unabashed by the fact.) But after some years this lucky 'bwoot' had gradually to cut down the calls to every other night or so. I found these long talks, many of them about things that could easily have waited till we met, a drain on my vitality at the end of a day.

Eleanor was a great one for detail. If she told you anything it was all recounted with absolutely nothing left out. And generally in great excitement at high speed and in forceful tones. I must say at once that when she used her voice ordinarily in serious conversation it was a pleasant one; and no observant person could fail to notice her hands. When I remarked on them, she told me that a poet (Margaret Radford) had once likened them to 'new milk'. It was a poet's description and apt—they were pale, smooth, soft: gentle, healing hands that could inflict no wounds.

As to cats: Eleanor was famous for her love of cats. Marmalade cats ('we don't like *ginger*'). She had been a woman of many cats, but by the time I caught up with her she had only one—Coney, the subject of one of her best books, *Golden Coney*. This cat was fifteen years old then, in 1950, and within a few weeks of my first visit to Hampstead Coney died.

Eleanor took it as she took most things, although she must have grieved inwardly, with a calm, realistic attitude. Life was life to her and when death came—well, it was time to go.

Two or three years later another cat arrived—Mr. Benignus Malone, named after our friend, Father Benignus, and the Mrs. Malone of Eleanor's poem. He was known eventually as Benny. He was a stray, found by Mrs. Herbert Farjeon. This minute marmalade kitten walked straight into our hearts. I became genuinely fond of Benny, but I am only a normal lover of cats. I do not think they should be spoiled. Eleanor was an abnormal cat-lover, and would have denied herself anything to meet her cat's needs. I believe I'm not exaggerating when I record that I have, on occasion, seen no less than three courses, all in a row, awaiting Benny's fanciful pleasure.

I am thankful to say Eleanor never talked baby-talk to her cats, or used a special animal voice. She treated them with respect and addressed them normally as she would have spoken to human beings.

Benny and I ultimately had to preserve a sort of armed neutrality. I loved him but sometimes found the fuss made of him a little hard to take. Benny, on his side, didn't bear me any grudge or resist my strokings and pettings. But he was jealous. He resented the change in the curriculum when I was staying there. Ordinarily he slept on Eleanor's bed, and could come and go through the sitting-room out into the garden and back again during the night hours. But this was disturbing to me, who slept in the sitting-room and was a very light sleeper. So at week-ends Benny was put downstairs with a window open to his nocturnal purposes. His anxious, interested look at my suitcases when I brought them down on

Sunday evenings prior to my departure was worth seeing. And if I dared to stay an extra night the signs of Benny's disapproval were unmistakable.

Eleanor as the lover of animals is most evident in 'Mrs. Malone.' She told me she considered this poem to be one of her best—of that kind of poem at any rate. She was pleased with it technically, of its deftness, its subtle alliterations and the easy way it ran. She told me that Viola Meynell had said that the ingenious management of the extra word in the last two lines 'made' the poem. 'Mrs. Malone' was a great favourite with audiences, to judge by its reception when Margaret Rutherford included it in a poetry programme, and on another occasion when I heard it done beautifully by Catherine Lacey.

The character of the old woman was plainly a projection of Eleanor herself. She adored animals of every kind, not only cats, and I am quite sure she would have starved herself as Mrs. Malone did, rather than see any dumb creature go hungry. Indeed, strays could always be sure of a welcome and a bite in Eleanor's house. There was one particular black and white cat who looked what he was, a down-and-out. We called him Danny, after Dan, the boy who strayed and came back again in Louisa Alcott's *Little Men*. Unlike the beautiful and spotless Benny, he was unkempt and hideous to look upon. I found it hard to like him. Not so Eleanor: for many years she left a plate of food for him in a special place where he knew he could always find it. One day he came no more.

Is it going over the edge of sentiment, I wonder, to picture Eleanor arriving in the next world and, like Mrs. Malone,

hearing the faint echoes of those two lines which Viola
Meynell admired and Father Mangan spoke at her baptism?

'There's room for another
One, Mrs. Malone.'

Apart from its technical perfection this poem has an
innocence and simplicity which belongs to the childlike
element that was so strong in Eleanor. And yet her versatility
was remarkable. 'Her Infinite Variety' was the caption that
appeared above a review of one of her books by Sylvia Lynd.
This was no easy compliment from one woman writer to
another. It was the plain truth. Eleanor could write a story
of adult love such as *Love Affair*; a satire, using a classical
legend, in *Ariadne and the Bull*, which Naomi Royde-Smith
described as 'brilliant'; sonnets, tender and moving, in *First
and Second Love*; and the sophisticated verse of *Kings and
Queens* (in collaboration with Herbert Farjeon), or *Thoughts
of the Lady in the Background*, alive with *double entendre*, which
she contributed to *The Saturday Book* of 1963.

All these and countless others belong to the grown-up
Eleanor Farjeon; the wise, compassionate woman, whom
many dozens of worried people climbed the hill to Hampstead to consult, to ask for her guidance and consolation in
their perplexities.

But I should like to enlarge a little on what I have referred
to more than once as 'the childlike element' in Eleanor; that
psychological aspect which, I feel, provides the explanation of
her power and magic, especially in her children's work.

From close and constant observation over many years I

came to the conclusion that Eleanor Farjeon was in some degree a split personality. Not in the Jekyll and Hyde meaning of the term, because in her case both persons were good; but in the Dr. Dodgson and Mr. Carroll sense. So that, just as if the author of *Alice in Wonderland* in his early days had been exposed to the analyst's microscope we should never have known the delight of that Looking-Glass World, so we should have been robbed of *Martin Pippin in the Apple Orchard* and the stories that went to make up *The Little Bookroom*, if the young Nellie Farjeon had been dissected and pulled to pieces by the psychiatrists.

There was nothing Nellie disliked more than being pulled to pieces. She was always insistent that there was a special compartment of her interior self that was private ground, and was not to be trespassed upon by even her closest friends. This came out very early, as she testifies in *A Nursery in the Nineties*, where, as a small child, she objected violently to having her bumps told; and again as an old woman, when she explained the exceptional reserve of a fellow-writer: "I understand her. She doesn't want to be *fingered*."

Neither did Eleanor Farjeon want to be fingered. This applies especially to her creative work. There were many occasions when she would be discussing some aspect of it in connection with a book she was writing, and she would break off abruptly with, "But I don't want to talk about it." She knew that the spells she wove were conjured up by a secret alchemy of her own which by analysis could only too easily be dispelled.

That alchemy belonged to Nellie, not to Eleanor. It had

its roots in the far-off days of the 'Nineties, when little Nellie
played a mysterious game in the nursery with her brother,
Harry. She described this in great detail in the *Nursery* book:
the never-ending fantasy life that went on even into their
adult years. They called it 'playing TAR'.

'. . . Harry says, "We'll have half-an-hour of TAR. Where
did we get up to?" Nellie tells him. They begin. An episode
of particular thrill is in progress. Nellie, for the moment
not herself, but M. le Comte de Guiche, or Hermia, or
Prince Ravna, for twenty-five minutes is rapt away from
earth, while she and Harry walk round and round the table,
talking and being, suffering and rejoicing. When they get
giddy, he wheels and walks the other way, and Nellie
follows, scarcely aware of the change of motion. At five
minutes to nine, out comes the silver watch; Harry holds
it in his hand as they perambulate. Now Nellie is only half-
absorbed in one of her multitudinous Other Selves; in four
minutes, three minutes, two, in one more minute, the knell
will sound. Back goes the watch in the pocket. "We're
Harry-Nellie-Joe-and-Bertie! Goodnight, dear." . . .'

So the game ended for that evening and Nellie was brought
back by the family pass-word to her real identity. But the
game was to go on the next day, and the day after, and the
day after that; on into their grown-up life.

Eleanor often said that it went on too long, preventing her
from maturing as early as she should have done. But I believe
that it was to those long years of playing TAR, those hours of
being 'rapt away from earth . . . walking round and round
the table,' (like those other creative spirits, the Brontë sisters)

'absorbed in her multitudinous Other Selves'—I believe that it was to the constant and prolonged practice of this strange ritual of identification that we owe the wealth of prose and poetry that poured out from Eleanor when she once began to write. And I believe that it was the other half of the split personality that was writing; that the secret of Eleanor Farjeon was that when she wrote *it was little Nellie writing; writing as a small excited girl would write if she had the power to do so.*

Eleanor was always most insistent that she never wrote a book *for* children. Many times she said, "I didn't write Martin Pippin in the Apple Orchard as a children's book". This is no doubt why that book, her first best-seller, and all her writings were as much enjoyed by grown-ups as by the children for whom they appeared to be intended.

We can take for granted that this little Nellie appeared in other ways and at other times than just when she was writing. Her infectious love of Christmas of which I have already written, from the first cards that arrived to the last presents received and opened on Christmas Day with all a child's delight and love of a surprise, was one manifestation of little Nellie. Eleanor always insisted on 'a surprise', and for birthdays too. You couldn't fob her off with some easy present that was something she had already seen or been told about. "Oh," she would say in a tone of rejection, "I like a surprise." And a surprise there had to be. This was by no means easy and called for much thought and ingenuity, because by the time I knew Eleanor she seemed to have everything. Not only on festive occasions but all through the year presents of every kind were showered upon her.

I used to tell her that being in her house was like staying at Max Gate with Thomas Hardy. Visitors from every corner of the world; telegrams, expensive flowers, mechanical toys and musical boxes; animals (cats especially) and candies; adorers and gifts of every kind came pouring in, in an endless cavalcade through her doorway. No prima donna could have asked for more.

And it wasn't just because she was a celebrity. People really loved her and she loved them. I have never met a human being with what one might describe as an almost God-like capacity for truly loving so many people at once. This quality of Eleanor's gave you a little insight into that attribute of God which we find so difficult to grasp; his ability to love each of the countless millions of creatures he has made. I used to think that if Eleanor could feel so deeply and abidingly for such a vast number of people, I could just faintly imagine, within the sphere of infinity, what the love of God might be.

As far back as 1956, when I was writing *Finding My Way*, I see that I spoke in the same strain about Eleanor: '. . . I found her more truly Christian than anyone I knew. She has an almost unique capacity for really and truly and deeply loving a great number of people. And in a lesser sense, I think, she loves most of her fellow-beings, and is quite incapable of those hateful thoughts to which too many of us are subject from time to time.

'I wrote earlier of the attractiveness of goodness. In Eleanor one feels this attraction very strongly. She has a special quality of her own, which emanates warmth and sweetness and a kind of healing. . . . Eleanor is probably the most put-upon woman in the world. "But I *like* to be put-upon," she said to me one day . . . To reach the stage when you "like" to be put-upon is surely to have found the true spirit of Christianity.'

It is a tribute to the unchanging goodness of Eleanor's character that now I come to write again about her after many more years of close friendship I should find myself saying, without first having referred to my former book, the same sort of things, and in words not dissimilar to those I used when my knowledge of her was less complete.

This section began with telephones and cats. Let it end with cats. A cat; the one and only Benny whom Eleanor and I both together loved. This is a fragment from a letter that I had from Eleanor and tore off to keep for reasons that will be plain:

'. . . Benny leapt in on my afternoon rest on the couch, chirruped at me, and bounded past to the corner of your bed, where he has curled and coiled for the last two hours—
    And so we lie and long for you,
    And pray that naught goes wrong for you,
    With spiritual Causeries
    On Thirty-days and Rosaries.
                God bless you,
                I love you,
                    Your Nell
                        X
                Funny without you.

CHAPTER FOURTEEN

ON THE BACK of the fragment of letter with which the last chapter finished I found a vivid piece of 'reporting' by Eleanor of day-to-day events.

The first broken paragraph refers to a visit she paid to the Piccadilly Theatre once again; this time to see a performance of her own delightful play written in collaboration with Herbert Farjeon, *The Two Bouquets*, which had been revived by Lord Vivian. Laura, one of the two leading girls, was played and sung most beautifully by Sonia Williams, whom Eleanor had met with me in *The White Sheep of the Family* Company.

'. . . next door to Sara's [Gregory], where a small drinking party was to take place for which he [Lord Vivian] had brought bottles. Everybody was there, and we had a gay half-hour. Sonia was amused and interested to hear about The White Sheep television, with a tinge of nostalgia when she heard you and Jack [Hulbert] and Derek [Blomfield] were to be in it. She was lovelier than ever in the piece; I told her how immensely womanly Laura had become, and she said, "I'm always finding more and more things in her to do." Yes, I do think it's a very nice show. . .'

Wednesday

'. . . This morning Geoffrey Wooley rang up and invited

me to "Norma" at Covent Garden tomorrow night. This old opera hasn't been done here for years—it was a great one with certain Divas a hundred and more years ago, and it is the opera I chose for Pierre and Denise to see in my play. [The play called *Pierre and Denise*.] One of the first-act scenes is in an opera-box à la Renoir . . .'

The revival of *The Two Bouquets* was, as usual, a joyous time for Eleanor. Nothing gave her greater happiness than to have a play running. She loved the human contacts, the visits to the theatre, looking in on people in their dressing-rooms. Actors and actresses are given to respond to that kind of friendliness. Playwrights are generally too shy to venture much behind the scenes during the run and in the rehearsal period inclined to be lost in the cavernous darkness of the shrouded stalls. Not so with Eleanor, although she always knew the right moment to make her presence felt and never played the tiresome author with a producer.

She would say that most of all she enjoyed the rehearsal period, when everything was in the making and she saw a great deal of the company. As to the first night of her own play, there was never any of the usual anxiety of a play-wright; it was just another Christmas party for Nellie.

The revival of *The Two Bouquets* and Eleanor's letter from which I quoted belong to 1953. In that year and the one previous to it there are many letters written to me by her which I hope to reproduce in this chapter.

There is a minute note written after a long Easter holiday, Eleanor's first Easter since she had become a Catholic:

Easter 1952

Till I die I shall try to say thank you—and afterwards I shall know how to—for this week, beyond all words.

I treasure that letter and the one that follows because they are proof of the fact that, despite the weepings and lamentations and the troubling of the waters of Eleanor's life that appear only too clearly in these pages, I can sincerely feel that I was able at the same time to give her happiness.

March 13th 1953

The Little Woman Round the Corner has done your cushions; she firmly scrapped everything on the backs, "a sort of horrible pink," said she, and hopes that what she has replaced it with is satisfactory. I'm sending her the pillow measurements and your stuff, which she will wash, and when that is done she hopes you can drive up and fetch everything, as the cushions will be difficult to post. I told her you wouldn't be coming here till next Thursday, but if you keep in touch with her you can arrange your own time. You can't expect *me* to arrange your dates with Little Women Round the Corners.

I've been writing you wonderful letters-in-the-head since yesterday; I wish I could write them as I think them. It was so lovely, like a human postscript to last Sunday's spiritual pastoral letter. We then had all that a Priest can give to our souls; and after the reaction (which I realise was almost inevitable) came the comfort of what a friend can do for our hearts and minds. Quiet warm happiness seemed to gather through the hours, and I don't know how to be glad enough of such a friend, or thankful enough to you for coming to give and take in that healing way. This, of course, is one of the things you or I will be bound to feel as a loss when one of us plays Annie over the other. If you go first, be sure *now* that every night and morning, and often at other times, the prayers for you will be part of my continuing here of our lovely friendship till my own time comes; and your bequest to me of Renée and Alban and John will be as much for my comfort as theirs. I'll do and be to them all I can, all they can let me be. If *I* go first, there's nobody of that sort to bequeath to you, except yourself. Take care of him for me, won't you? With God's help always. And mine, however that may be.

This question of death and purgation (By the way, did you see the Catholic Herald on Stalin?—comfort for Alban and all of us). I've been thinking how, since Absolution obliterates for that instant all our sins, if we die in that Grace we go *almost* ready to God; but if we had not died, if we had recovered after the Viaticum, we should still, though freed of sin, carry the nature that is capable of sin; and it is that *nature*, isn't it, that has to be purged in all of us (except the Saints themselves) since the capability of frailty cannot possibly be carried with us to heaven. That is what we must all undergo; but without trying to minimise what this may mean, I am sure it is not what we imagine when we think of, and dread it, in the terms of human tortures. I have a feeling that it is not the infliction of pain, but the removal of the evil that causes pain—the removal of a tremendous spiritual splinter that, as long as we live, may fester and give us trouble. The removal itself may hurt, as it is parted from us, but it is not a harsh act directed upon us by God; only the last tremendous act of His infinite mercy. I *cannot* fear God, I am utterly confident of Him, and after death what I am is wholly in His hands. *Before* death I must continue to fear myself, of myself I can't be confident; and continual repenting and continual trying is all I can do, after continual failing. Well, my beloved Denys, that is the same for all of us, some of us sin more than others, fail oftener, and try less; but His love is as absolute for the failures and the sinners as for the Saints. Love has no qualifications, though we poor human creatures have so many. But if our efforts are continually towards Him, I am sure we need not terrify ourselves ("like children in the dark") with thoughts of a Hell we cannot even conceive. My-death/Your-death. Don't be frightened, darling. I know your goodness. If you knew it, it would be less.

I like this in the Collect today: "As in our body we abstain from food, so may we fast from sin in our mind." And I liked all that beautiful water flowing about in the Lesson and in the Gospel, and thought of you drinking glassfuls of it with your meals. And I thought what you said about cleanliness and washed my hair and had a special go at Little Nellie's Nails . . .

Death, purgatory, hell, heaven. We should 'Never be done with talking', Eleanor and I, indeed. Nor writing either, apparently, round about this time. The next letter of Eleanor's suggests that the graph on the chart above my head had been a good deal steadier. "The Love that makes a fool of Himself . . ." is a quotation from Father Benignus, who played a big part in Eleanor's consciousness.

July 23rd 1953

You must have a letter to tide you over these three days (though *one never knows!*) I can't describe the lightness of heart you have left me with; but perhaps you have only to look inside to see its reflection. Happiness is very catching. I wish you could see what it is doing for you as I've seen it these last few days, and others will. This miracle of happiness, that I believe is going to change immensely the rest of your life, hasn't happened as suddenly as seems. It is the result of growing-up pains and sufferings, through which you have never really given up, have always tried even in your despairs—so God has helped you to help Him in all His love would do for you. If the prayers of us who love you so much have helped too, it is only by going up to Him and returning from Him to you, *because* you never stopped trying. You have done it yourself—in the end it must always be so for each of us. By ourselves, with God. That is the true security which the death of those we love, who have prayed for us, cannot shake. Dear Denys, the prayers will go on always, the love which inspired them is part of the miracle, for that too is from God. So that we can almost *see* it in our lives, in those with whom we share it— You—John—Me, Me-You—John, John-You-Me—a faint but clear reflection of the Love that "makes a fule of Himself for ye". You cannot help realising it (Him) in the heart of your Faith if you realise us, its lesser form in the heart of your life. As I feel, with joyful certainty, you do.

But we won't leave a loophole. There's all the way to go, all the time. We'll go on watching, and trying, and praying, and loving, and rejoicing. And thanking, thanking, thanking God for the gift of each other through whom to realise Him . . .

Later, in high summer, an even happier letter from Eleanor dealing with no particular problems, but very expressive of her joyous self:

Aug. 11th 1953

I do hope things weren't too fretted for you (my verb) after you got back to heat and dust and noise and Marys and things. It is odd how your going leaves a gap in this place. No, it isn't a bit odd. I've had a good rest-of-the-morning in the Garden Room, getting the script to Cusack, writing for Ada's "character" and all-sorts. Now I'll settle down to Dickens after a lettuce-and-banana sort of lunch and get near the finish of him. I'd like to be able to cry "All done!" when you come on Friday. The open doorway is full of sunflower in the sun, with hollyhocks above and roses beyond. Benny has been in, told me it's too hot to eat, and gone out again. And somewhere—upstairs on the couch or round the corner on Blakelock's Perch—*you* ought to be. But I'm not pining; with that power of enjoyment I wish you could share with me, *it's lovely missing you.* Well, it *would* be a loss if I didn't! Anything one can do with all one's heart is worth while—and I miss you with all mine. There'll be many prayers added to the Treasury before you get this. Oh, how I hope you've waked up happy . . .

(The reference to Dickens: Eleanor was writing a Fore-word to a new edition of *A Christmas Carol.*)

And in November a more serious letter again. It sounds as if irritability on my part, followed by morbid self-reproach and profuse apology, had spoiled that visit. Eleanor, as usual, goes more than halfway to make it all right; not only for that moment, but for any likely feeling of remorse laid up for later on.

Nov. 25th 1953

Death may come slowly and expectedly, or quickly and too suddenly to be foreseen; and the last moment one has shared with a beloved friend—with every friend, in fact— may easily not have been perfect. If I go out on some such moment for you, you must remember that it, and any other moments that might grieve you in remembrance, are the merest grains of sand under the sea, not to be known or seen, only forgotten. Love is perfect, and takes the beloved whole, beyond the imperfections: as I do You. They are such *nothings*, Denys darling, in loving-friendship. We bring our whole selves to this relationship, our best and our second-best and all the degrees below these to our worst. We can't suddenly be relieved of our imperfections, our special failings, because we love. Only Christ's love can do that utterly in a moment, if He and we will. The rest of us, in whom by His grace the Holy Spirit moves, help and are helped by those we love through it. That is what God lets us do for each other here. You do not *know* what you do for me—nor I what I do for you, darling. We *do* know that we are sharing something beyond our human littlenesses. They can't even prick or scratch it. If you die first I shall never remember your irritabilities, or waste time and spirit on self-reproach for the times I've failed you by being this or that. If I die first, you won't. What we shall leave with each other for continual comfort and strength is not to be touched by the conscience-twinges with which the Devil attempts to poison our pure grief. Of course we shall grieve, but the Comforter will do His part for both of us. While He is doing it, say clearly to yourself, "I never hurt her." It is the truth.

And one more letter, another happy one this time, with which to end a chapter.

Dec. 15th 1952

What happened from Saturday teatime onwards was wonderful. I've been thanking God for it ever since—for the blooming of such lovely feelings in you, tenderness for X, love and understanding of Keats, the creative feelings in one's heart instead of the destructive ones; instead of hate and anger, love and compassion—the only answers to it all, in the end. Oh I do love you so deeply and dearly Denys. I am always glad of you, but I have seldom been so glad for you.

CHAPTER FIFTEEN

IT MUST BE evident by now that Eleanor Farjeon was no ordinary woman. At this point I should like to write a little more fully about the fancies and foibles and unexpected oddities which did not in any way detract from Eleanor's likeability, but on the contrary only served to make her the more human and endearing, more individual and amusing.

"Really Eleanor, you are *extraordinary*! On the one hand you . . . on the other . . ."

"Yes, I'm a mass of inconsistencies." She said this defiantly and obviously gloried in it.

She was a character unexpected, unpredictable and perverse, though the last word could be misleading. Eleanor was fundamentally too kind and too unselfish to be deliberately perverse. But I used sometimes to say, "It's just like living with Maria Callas."

She was never temperamental in a stormy way, or caused suffering to those around her. Nevertheless, she could be described as now up, now down, with always a *crise* on hand, of her own or of someone else's. Gervase Farjeon's words come to my mind once again: "Drama has always gone on round Nellie."

I was to learn more and more how true this was much later on when our friendship went through rather a dark time; and as she grew older and less well.

As an example of her tendency to play the actress: Eleanor did indeed suffer badly from the combination of heavy build and maladjusted feet; but one could not help noticing quite early on that her sense of drama would take over and she would rather overdo the cripple with the walking-stick, hobbling along and leaning heavily on her escort. John McBennett has an amusing story of accompanying her to Covent Garden. In the interval she tottered to the buffet, supported by his strong right arm. Suddenly she realised the bar bells had gone and the curtain was about to rise. At the thought of missing a moment of her beloved opera, all infirmities were forgotten. She turned and without stick or arm ran like a young woman down the passage to her seat.

In the home, had Eleanor married and had a family, she would undoubtedly have been a great matriarch. She was certainly a powerful housewife and prided herself on the way she ran her house as regards the management of the kitchen and the commissariat. She knew about food and wine and was a wonderful cook. In her eighties she really enjoyed cooking and busying herself about the kitchen. Once there, she donned a voluminous blue apron in which she had something of the air of a beaming Breton peasant woman, a description which I think she would have liked. Eleanor owed much of her knowledge of cooking to her visits to France with Pod, where she would strike up a friendship with a hotel chef and be given personal demonstrations downstairs in the kitchen regions.

One of Eleanor's best broadcast talks, which were always

admirable, was the one she did on Woman's Hour, *Omelette at Chinon*. Her omelettes were delicious.

Although in one way Eleanor Farjeon lived in a muddle, on the other hand she was extremely able and well-organised. In the kitchen there was a place for everything and everything was in its place.

Upstairs, in her sitting-room and bedroom, there was a place for everything and nothing was in its place. That is to say from the onlooker's point of view. She herself knew pretty well where things were to be found, and could not bear you to move a single paper. "I can find my own way amongst my own muddle," she would say. And what a muddle it was too, the sitting-room. Such disorder, such congestion: packed to the wainscoting with an immense and formless conglomeration of chairs, cupboards, tables, standing bookshelves, hanging bookshelves, a radio and a record player; and, on the large table at which she worked, piles of books, papers, files, unanswered letters, pens, ink, and biros by the dozen, and of course the inevitable typewriter—several.

This was the room in which I slept and found cosy though claustrophobic. But Eleanor loved that room as she loved no other, and it was the only place in which she could write. Atmosphere made an enormous difference to her. She said she could not have written, for instance, in my large, light room in Bayswater, where I went to live in 1963. She preferred a room that was crowded and rather dark; and particularly one that had sloping roofs. A sort of glorified attic, in fact, was what she liked best as a workroom. She always wrote and re-wrote in long-hand, with many typewritten drafts to follow, before she finally sent her copy to a professional typist.

Eleanor had tremendously high standards. Her father's influence and example in such matters remained with her all her life. 'Children, be good to your mother and to each other. Do your duty in life, and use your talents worthily.' He wrote these words on a sheet of paper found by Eleanor after his death. She lived up to what he would have wished of her to the end.

After her fifth operation and convalescence she returned to the manuscript of her own Memoir, which she had worked on in 1962 and much of which she had read to me. I thought it excellent, and that a great deal of it was Eleanor's writing at its best. But it disappointed and worried her. "Why don't you show it to your publisher and ask him what he thinks?" I said. "No," Eleanor replied, "He might like it—and it's got to satisfy *me*."

She told me she could never send out inferior material just because she was under contract to a publisher. It had to come up to her own exacting standards.

All this, and the record of her output of well over eighty books alone, fits in oddly with the fact that she told me once that she had a tendency to slothfulness. I was surprised, as she seemed in every way to be such an active person. And yet later I began to see that there was some truth in this self-accusation.

Eleanor loved her bed; and any excuse to stay in it could be welcome. Which leads me on to another aspect of her character: her capacity for a certain kind of self-deception. She was an extrovert and not given to probing into her own motives. This showed itself in a rather endearing way when she became a Roman Catholic, in the matter of the obligation to hear Mass on Sundays.

The priest she met through me, and after whom she named her cat, Father Benignus, C.P., unwittingly gave her a watertight and permanent dispensation. He said that, when she felt bronchitic or could not climb the hill, she could then 'send her heart to Mass.'

From that moment on, Eleanor took disarming and childlike advantage of these merciful words of comfort, given to an ageing woman whose parish church was set on a high hill. But she wasn't then that old, and she had superabundant vitality—one of her Jewish inheritances—for doing the things she wanted to do. She once sat right through *The Ring*, for instance, during the week but, when Sunday came, she sank back on her pillows and said, "I think I'll send my heart to Mass today."

Even when she had had a normally quiet week at home, I could not fail to notice that often on a Saturday night she began to feel less well; or that, as late as Sunday morning itself, she would decide to send her heart to Mass.

Yet she genuinely loved going and felt deprived later when she really could not go, even in the car with me. It was just a human weakness—the slothful tendency she had long ago recognised in herself. Sometimes the comfort of the bed pulled too hard.

CHAPTER SIXTEEN

THE YEAR 1954 was going to be an important one. I was to make a decision, to take a step that would affect Eleanor and me in many ways undreamed of. Since, at the age of seventeen, I had decided to abandon medicine for the theatre, it was the most far-reaching decision of my life.

In that spring I was asked to play, in Sir John Gielgud's production of *The Cherry Orchard*, the part of Firs, the ancient coachman. Those who saw this character played by the Russian actor at Sadlers Wells a few years ago will not find it difficult to recall. I accepted the engagement and found myself rehearsing once again at the Haymarket Theatre. I liked the rôle and was already beginning to feel that sense of interior identification with the character which always made even me hopeful of success with the part I was playing.

In a mood of fatal optimism I worked on Firs for several days, but soon the familiar sense of uneasiness set in. At four o'clock one morning, after an almost sleepless night, I decided to throw in my hand, and that this time it must be for good. I wrote a letter of explanation to John Gielgud and walked down through the quiet streets to leave it and the script with the fireman at the Haymarket stage door.

As I walked home again I realised I had taken a fatal step and wondered what lay ahead. Although I had found little happiness on the stage, acting had appeared to be my vocation all those years. With my usual probings I wondered if I had done a weak thing in turning my back on it at a comparatively early age. But as the time went by I was to see very clearly that all this was meant to be; that the coming to a crossroad, where a change of direction seemed the only choice, was all part of the itinerary. I was to find that it was possible to have more than one vocation in life, and that, as he often seems to do, Almighty God, by the force of practical circumstances, had made my way plain.

Judging from a short letter I had had from Eleanor earlier in the year I must have been working up to this for some weeks.

Jan. 3rd 1954

I have prayed for you a great deal in the night, without any question why you must suffer as you do, or any doubt that God when He pleases can relieve the suffering. Now I am going to offer my Mass for you and light candles for you, and all through this day there will be many more prayers for you. At this small distance, while you are going through whatever the day brings, you will be surrounded —and shielded, I pray—by everything that love can do for you through prayers and through God.

Dear Denys, may today weary you *only* in body, and leave your tired mind and nerves in peace. May you sleep quietly tonight. I love you humanly past telling and in God past understanding.

However, I am glad to see from another longer letter from her that I was not only and all the time thinking of my own troubles. I was by no means lacking in considerable concern for Eleanor's in hers.

Feb. 3rd 1954

Your concern for me is my dear comfort, and infinitely precious to me, and little as I want to distress my friends and relatives in general about the less easy things in my life, your distress for them (as mine for yours) is a part of the whole wonderful *caring* between you and me for whatever affects the other in our profound loving-friendship. I wouldn't have you un-distressed entirely, that's asking for an impossibility, and I would never withhold any sort of confidence from you for that reason; but I would always, if possible, relieve the stress of the distress for you by keeping you aware of my compensations. A thing to remember, as one grows old, with the inevitable waning of all sorts of the powers of one's prime, is Samuel Butler's advice to eat one's grapes downwards, so that one is always eating the best on the bunch—even if it is not quite so fine as the grape one ate yesterday. (I am turning his actual bunch of grapes into a metaphor, but as Pod's father told him: "Consider the nature of the metaphor, there is nothing else"—i.e. in the realm of Truth.) So, I am enjoying my sight downwards, and every day know that I have, and can use, the best of what's left; and when I consider the people who are totally blind, and know what a treasure of sight is still mine for use, and what a good grape there is still on the bunch, when I can look out of my windows (as I do now) on the sunlit backs of Church Row, through a lacework of leafless trees, and the clear, blue sky above the roofs. And I *can* read, and I *can* work, and even when I abuse my eyes now and then in the work, I have the tremendous compensation of the feeling of something accomplished. So a bit of a headache in consequence doesn't distress me half as much as it does you for me.

I have often thought how the dependence of old age, because of waning powers, comes full circle with the helplessness of infancy while the powers are waxing. The state of *Not-Being-Able-To* can be as irking to one as to the other. The difference is that the child is straining to become independent while the old one is straining not to lose independence. No healthy being really wants—or ought to want—anybody else to be responsible for him, but in extreme youth and old age it can't be helped (or of course in extreme illness at any age). But the child is unaware of the burden that responsibility lays on its mother, who accepts it as a portion of her life (and is too seldom wise enough to know when to shift the load). The old one brings an adult awareness to the problem, and to know how to grow dependent without being a nuisance is one of the last bits of wisdom life asks of us. As for those who have to assume responsibility at both ends of the scale, they too must be wise enough to let the young and the old take their own risks; a completely protected life is hardly worth living. I shall never regret leaving Pod unconstrained to do the garden-jobs which were his delight, and which led to his last tumble. He could have tumbled for a less good reason than a pot of flowers for the garden, God bless him.

After all this generalising, let me come back to my own particular, and promise you that the idea of losing my hearing would be far far more serious to me than the idea of losing my sight. My life is my friends, much more than my work; and of all my friends, you. No seeing takes the place of sound and touch, and while I can hear your voice and take your hand I have the very best grape on the bunch.

So Eleanor was moving into her more difficult years at the same time as I was going forward into a different, quieter and happier way of life.

The first thing I did, after laying down my grease paints for the last time, was to retrieve my position at the Royal Academy of Dramatic Art, where I had just refused an offer to give my usual classes during the Summer Term, owing to the engagement in *The Cherry Orchard*. I returned that May to the R.A.D.A. under Sir Kenneth Barnes, picked up my class register and began a teaching life with a new sense of purpose and vocation.

In this Eleanor took the keenest interest, providing me with material for dramatic studies, coming to the performances, and concerning herself in personal ways with many of the students. And when, a year later, our old friend John Fernald, producer of *The Silver Curlew* and *The White Sheep*, took over from Sir Kenneth, Eleanor was brought more and more into the Academy life, at least two of her plays being performed by the students under the new régime.

So I practised on Peter O'Toole, Albert Finney and many others now famous; for I found that one has to *learn* to teach.

Just as I was to find from Eleanor Farjeon that one has to learn to write; and that it takes half a lifetime, not just a tenth of one, to do so. For writing, mainly for the theatre, was the other fork of the two-pronged vocation to which I turned in 1954; both concurrently with each other, and both at exactly the same time as I renounced the theatre as an actor. It was early in Easter Week that I resigned from *The Cherry Orchard*, so that it was at the end of the Easter holiday that I began my drama teaching career in earnest; and it was over the Easter weekend that I wrote my first two poems under Eleanor's roof, and under her influence and encouragement that I went on writing them, and then more, and then many more, until I had spilled up out of myself, with varying degrees of merit as poems, all the perilous stuff that had collected in my bosom over fifty years. It was a great catharsis.

Although at first the verses were simple, naïve and inevitably religioso, I eventually found my way, as I had found it in the theatre, into my own field—the comedic. Within three years of those small beginnings I had the first of two long, satirical poems accepted by John Hadfield for *The Saturday Book*, and illustrated by Ronald Searle.

In all this Eleanor Farjeon, with unwearying patience, put at my disposal her great talents, knowledge and experience. To the axiom about the writing of poetry given me by Walter de la Mare, Eleanor added many more. She began by saying there were of course rules for the poet; and that there were also *no* rules. But that you must know what the rules were before you could break them. Free verse was only safe for one who had known the chains of discipline.

These are a few of the rules which Eleanor gave me:

(i)   The half is more than the whole:
(How effective is understatement.)

(ii)   To be very sparing with one's adjectives:
(Eleanor used to quote what D. H. Lawrence said to her: 'I would compel a young writer to put down 500 words without using a single adjective.' Then he added: 'Unless of course he wanted to describe a negro with red hair.')

(iii)   To be equally sparing with one's exclamation marks:
(My early attempt at an autobiography, which Eleanor had tried to lick into shape, had been peppered with them. Never use them to show the reader how funny your joke is supposed to be.)

(iv)   A poem is not a matter of inspiration and nothing more; it has to be worked on—sometimes for hours —for days.
(Dorothy Wordsworth, in her Journals, describes her brother as getting agitated over 'working on' a poem.)

(v)   When one writes a ballad poem or a satirical verse it must be 'deft' (a favourite word of Eleanor Farjeon's). It must run and flow with consummate ease.

(vi)   That 'false' rhymes, such as 'dawn' and 'born' are frowned upon by all good poets.

And finally, Eleanor taught me much about the shaping of a book; the art of selection and the 'management' of material. In the poetry-writing phase, which went on in an intense degree for about a year and a half, I would speak each poem to Eleanor and she would give me her immediate emotional reaction to it. Then she would read it to herself and point out its technical faults. Less often in the early days I would send her a poem by post and she would write about it to me, as shown by these two letters written in January 1955. The first is from me:

> Here it is and I think and hope you'll approve. But don't hesitate to say so if you don't. Thank you, dearest, for sparing me a bit of your poor eyes for my poor poems.
>
> You will be a grass widow this week-end. What an opportunity! I did feel the other afternoon what an ego-centric menace I'd been. Telling you of all my incurable vanities—my reactions to Joyce Redman's letter and Peggy's [Margaretta Scott] etc. That yellow rose and I are awful—we deserve to lose our leaves.
>
> But you know, I don't really think much of myself, and I do know that my 'talent' for poetry writing is a very small one. And anyway, it's only the Holy Spirit playing TAR.

And this from Eleanor:

> In case we don't speak tonight, as you may be back late from your outing, I want to tell you at once that Winter Wings is one of your best. In about half-a-dozen lines a word (or syllable) seems unnecessary to the rhythm when I have read it aloud; but today I'll read and re-read it until I'm fairly sure of what *I* think might be better, always, of course, deferring to the author. But you musn't, to make it suitable to be read in public by a man, alter it. Poems are

male, or female (or, of course, neuter); this is a female poem, and must remain so. The other little poem is a dear and lovely tribute. I think there is a slight gain in dropping "That" out of line 3; and I *think*, I think, there is a gain in dropping the "this" in the last line but one. But read it aloud and see if you agree.

And here is darling Clare's Gull for you again. [A sketch by Clare Leighton] I am writing to her today.

And here is dear Terry's letter. [Terence Knapp] I'm not at all surprised that anyone so young and affectionate can relax more in a letter than in a talk. The young, who may seem so confident, aren't always as confident as they seem, and there may be a faint camouflage of being-at-ease which affects things. What is sweet is that he can, and wants to, express affection when he writes; without being explicit the warmth is in the air of the letter.

And it is in the air of your very dearest letter to *your* Nell; it made her extremely happy, especially as she was feeling little-Nellish after finding and reading aloud the Christmas-party script for the 25th.

'That yellow rose' in my letter refers to a poem which I wrote called 'Vain Thought of a Rose'. There *had* to be poems about roses of course.

> Buds thought the rose,
> Buds, never to burgeon forth ...

and

> White rose, climbing in such profusion over the
> high barn ...

And leaves too:

> The leaves are lying, lying on the ground,
> The green is dying, dying all around . . .

There were a lot of leaves in my first poems and they were all dead or dying.

At the same point when I started to take classes at the Academy, I also began to coach private pupils in my own home. This in a small way and for a small fee, as I did not then consider myself justified in asking more as an untrained and inexperienced instructor. That side of my teaching life steadily built itself up until eventually I often found myself with more pupils than I wanted.

Although most of the private ones consisted of drama students and stage aspirants, a great many came from other walks of life and they were the most interesting of all, just because they provided such a change of experience. Chinese Law students, Big Business men, a Cabinet Minister, a thriving Covent Garden produce merchant, a famous pop-singer, a Jewish Rabbi, a top-crust soldier wrestling with a funeral panegyric to be spoken in the presence of Royalty. There was a steady stream of them, each with their problem (often psychological) of speech, of manner, of self-presentation.

Eleanor Farjeon took the greatest interest in this, as in every aspect of my new life; and many of my private pupils, as well as those from the R.A.D.A., found their way up to her house; even if it were only to have a session with me in the Garden Room which she let me use for emergency lessons at the weekends.

The publication over eleven years of my four successful books for theatre students and an autobiography was a great joy, as well as being a growing surprise, I think, to Eleanor. She accepted me at last as a fellow professional and went so far in 1965 as to say, "It's funny, isn't it? I seem to have trained you up to be my biographer."

It was the greatest compliment she could pay me to trust me blindly to do this book, which she never saw because she said, "I don't like seeing myself in the looking-glass."

CHAPTER SEVENTEEN

IT WAS THE summer of 1955. Everything in the garden was lovely; Eleanor's garden which I shared with her. A new happiness had come to me, a new interest in life. This poem by W. H. Davies, discovered for me by Eleanor round about that time, expresses exactly my feelings as they were then. Could I have been capable of writing such poetry, these lines might well have been written by me about myself:

My Youth

My youth was my old age,
    Weary and long;
It had too many cares
    To think of song;
My moulting days all came
    When I was young.

Now, in life's prime, my soul
    Comes out in flower;
Late, as with Robin, comes
    My singing power;
I was not born to joy
    Till this late hour.

In this late hour I too had found peace and seemed to be learning to possess my soul in quiet. And on Eleanor's side I think I provided a background of security for one who was getting old, had lost many of her dearest relatives and friends of her own generation, and the man she had loved for so many years.

But things seldom work out as simply as that. 'Living happily ever after' belongs to the world of Fairy Tales and has little to do with life as we have to face it realistically. The last paragraphs of my autobiography had been written on a note of renunciation and resignation, of all passion spent. It was frequently to occur to me that, were I to write another book dealing with my life from that moment onwards, I might well call it, I Spoke Too Soon. The private world of D.B., that little, womb-safe world of immunity and unnatural peace was going to be split from top to bottom. Drama was once more about to be played round Nellie, and once again I unwittingly was to be the one responsible for it.

There are some things of which, even in these days of brash confession, it is not possible—for people like myself at any rate—to write in detail. It is enough to say that in that August of 1955 the pains and perplexities of an infatuation took hold of me: that sickness that turns a middle-aged man into a fool, without will-power, reason or dignity. There is no antidote, no antibiotic. The fever has to rage until it is spent. The attempt from love's sickness to fly is of no avail, and everything and everyone has to go down before it. So it was with me for the best part of seven years. This would have no place here, but for its disruptive repercussions on my friendship with Eleanor Farjeon, and the unsuspected depths in her which it revealed.

With an idiotic ingenuousness I made her the recipient of my endless confidences as I had always done, and as if she herself was quite detached from the circumstances surrounding them. It took a long and painful time for it to dawn on me that the security she had found so happily in our life together she now saw, not only imperilled, but perhaps even in the process of destruction.

I did my best. I still went up to Hampstead at the weekends. I still tried faithfully to keep up the constant telephone calls, which had continued over all those years. I strove to keep everything the same. But it is not possible for the human heart to be in one direction captivated and at the same time give more than token attention to the demands of a relationship which has become for the moment secondary. This dichotomy between conscience in one direction and overweening desire in another threatened my mental stability.

It seemed an impossible situation. I at least knew and understood the nature of my sickness, and had a psychiatrically-minded doctor and friend to help me face the truth. But Eleanor must have suffered deeply because the cause of her distress was hidden from her. She, who probably never before had known the pains of jealousy, had believed herself unpossessive and undemanding, and had never had to face the possibilities of such human weakness within, now found herself a prey to impulses up to then unknown.

All that I have written of in a few paragraphs occupied, as I have said, a stretch of about seven years. During those years the clock was put back for me. Only a short time before,

I had written confidently and all too prematurely, as if it were behind me for ever: 'I lived for years like one who knew there was a man-eating tiger in the basement with an insufficient lock on the door . . .' In the period of emotional disturbance which I am now describing, the tiger returned; and although in the immediate present things are quieter once more I should hesitate ever again to speak with such assurance.

At long last the infatuation died; and for myself alone not a moment too soon, for it had a profound effect on every department of my life. My powers of concentration became impaired. Over all that period I was constantly forgetting important matters, and missing appointments. I lost interest in my work, and to this day find it difficult to read a book.

I do not know how I may appear in all this to the dispassionate eye. I feel I continued to do my utmost, in not easy circumstances, to give as much happiness as I could to Eleanor who had given so much to me.

In the end my efforts and her patience were rewarded. Good, even, came out of this long protracted agony. It turned me into a relatively adult human being and the relationship which now re-formed itself became on my side far more mature and on hers perhaps more moderate.

Much later on, after one particularly happy week-end, I had an impulse to write her a letter, giving her the reassurance I instinctively felt she needed. Her reply, so typical of Eleanor, touched me deeply, and will always be a comfort to me and be read and read again.

September 3rd, 1963

... You've given me strength to go on, and assurance and comfort, more than you know.

Dearest, dearest Denys, *do* you think our loving-friend-ship doesn't owe as much to you as it does to me?

I rely on it as you do, and in the fulness of love you stand in my life with my three boys [brothers] with Edward, and with Pod.

X was something different—a shooting-star among the planets, bright, sudden and unforgettable. My sky holds up without him. If one of my six fell out of the sky the firmament would shake.

As for causes to be grateful, if I have helped your middle years a little, think what you do for my old ones. Or don't think . . . Just know that you make my old life worth living as nothing else does.

Along with that letter I treasure another one, written much earlier, during the period of re-adjustment.

May 16th 1960

I want you to be happy, I want it so much; I pray for it morning and night, and oftener; and when I'm praying for it I pray also for the clearing away of the things which seem to prevent it from day to day or week to week.

But though in our daily life these recurring trials may seem to us to be the obstacles to happiness, they are not really . . .

Our beloved Lord has shown you, as your most loving friends never could, where lasting happiness only can be—

in *ourselves*, while we live in continual touch with the Holy Spirit. While we realise this and the miracle of His example, we carry our untouchable source of happiness into the recurring human troubles. No mere clearing away of these is enough. They are made powerless when we stop fearing and hating them. That is what we have to fight in ourselves for Christ's sake. We have to do it again and again, as often as the world and the Devil strike at us, which in one way and another is every minute.

And of course we fail again and again; and then we must fight despair, the worst devil of all. That is when the Holy Spirit will never 'leave you down' [an Irishism used by a mutual friend]. I know now that you are nearer happiness than you have ever been.

As for me, what you rang up this morning to say makes this day happier than if Stallard [her oculist] had come and said I would see without glasses better than ever before.

Can you believe that I'd rather be blind, than that you should not be happy?

This letter I received round about the time when Eleanor had been through the ordeal of her second cataract operation. The last sentence was written in no passing mood of emotional exaltation. Eleanor may have been sentimental, but she was not given to that sort of unreality. I am quite certain she was capable of making that sacrifice. She would have accepted blindness, had she known that by doing so she could have brought peace of mind to me.

Can one ever be thankful enough for having met such a woman, and for having had the privilege of her friendship?

The X, in the first of these two letters, is someone of whom I cannot write. He gave Eleanor Farjeon the ardent love for which her romantic nature craved. It was innocent, short-lived, a brief encounter that must remain for ever undisclosed.

Her feeling for Pod, she told me, deep and lasting though it was, was more maternal than physical. As for Edward Thomas, there is no secret in the fact that he was the man she loved above all. But he was happily married and therefore could only give her his friendship in return. Eleanor loved them both, Helen and Edward, and spent a great deal of time with them and their children in the country. She was rightly outraged when, in a radio programme about the poet, it was implied that she had shared a *ménage à trois* with Edward Thomas and his wife. She insisted on that part being cut out of the tape when the programme was repeated.

Eleanor objected to it on two counts: it was not true, and she could never have agreed to such a design for living anyway.

CHAPTER EIGHTEEN

ONE BEAUTIFUL SUNDAY evening in 1959 we were sitting in the garden enjoying the still warm October sun. Eleanor was reading the paper and I was as usual day-dreaming. Suddenly she exclaimed and said, "Listen. How would this suit you?" Eleanor knew it was my great desire to find a house of my own up there near her and she was always scanning the house agents' advertisements on my account. She read out what Hamptons had to offer me: 'Old Hampstead five minutes shops and Underground charming studio residence for sale designed by famous architect bedroom kitchen bathroom parquet flooring minstrels' gallery walled garden with lily-pond. Freehold £6,500.'

The description collared me. I decided to go and have a look at the studio at the first possible moment. As usual the demon urgency seized hold of me and on that Sunday night I could hardly sleep for the anticipation of telephoning-time in the morning. By 9.30 a.m. I had been given an appointment to view the studio at midday. It proved to be on Windmill Hill, just below the Heath, at the back of Fenton House. It had been built in the 1930's to the designs of Sir Edward Maufe for Gluck, as she liked to be called, without the 'Miss'. Gluck was a painter and a rich woman who lived in one of the beautiful old houses on Holly Hill and the studio had been erected as a workroom at the bottom of her garden. When I described it later to Eleanor she remembered it well, having dined several times with Gluck before the war, she and Pod. After dinner they used to cross the garden, passing the lily-pond, and sit in the studio where they had coffee and talked into the night.

As I saw it on that morning the studio was fascinating. It was large and lofty and every inch of wall-space was taken up with unfinished canvases and brightly-coloured paintings and all the clobber of an artist's workshop. There was the musicians' gallery, along the south wall. The mellow sunlight of that glorious autumn morning was streaming through the small window at the back, and the vivid scarlet carpet on the white staircase leading up to the gallery captured my fancy at a glance. But it was the view of the studio from the garden that finally got me. Steps led down from French windows beneath a semi-circular epistyle, supported by two columns of Ionic design. And the peace of it! There wasn't a sound to be heard, and yet I knew that the shops and the Underground were only a few moves away. I was enchanted. I was enslaved. This demi-paradise was what I had been searching for for years.

With a few cursory enquiries and beseeching the owner to give me the first refusal, I swiftly left the house and made for my car trembling as with the ague. All my urgency rose to meet the situation and took control, banishing commonsense and caution. "I must have it, I *must* have it," I said, as I pressed the self-starter. And again, "I must have it," to Eleanor a few moments later. "You *shall* have it," she cried like the Fairy Godmother to Cinderella. This clinched it. I took up the telephone, dialled the house agent's number and bought the studio on the spot.

I looked at my watch. It was just about half an hour since I had first set eyes on the studio on Windmill Hill.

How I bought it, in three weeks regretted it, tried to sell it, in the end kept it and converted it, and one month after the house-warming sold it and returned to a one-roomed Bloomsbury flat—all this belongs to my own story, not to Eleanor's. Nevertheless, she was in on it from the beginning to the end, although she did not play such a big part in the events as usual, owing to the fact that during much of that period she was undergoing and recovering from her second cataract operation. In fact, she only came up to the house on two or three occasions, one of which was the house-warming. On that day she stayed put in an armchair on the same spot in the ground-floor studio room and the hundred odd guests rotated round her. During the conversion and moving-in period Eleanor housed many of my extravagant purchases in her Garden Room, and when I moved out she bought, or was given, a number of the things I was forced to get rid of.

It was a dark period between the house-warming and the moment when I made my decision to sell the Studio House, as I called it, and go back to central London. This poem which I wrote a few weeks later will to some extent explain the situation and illuminate the state of mind which led to behaviour so seemingly eccentric and impulsive. How, when one dreams and plans, can one always anticipate what the reality will be?

The House

I saw the house, I loved the house,
I bought it all too soon;
It seemed to look so lovely
In the shining Autumn noon.

The workmen came and made the house
A place of friendship ever;
The workmen went, but I remained;
I thought to leave it never.

The guests came too, and then the house
Was filled with warmth and laughter;
Guest and workman left the house,
Bereft from floor to rafter.

Only a ghost stayed in the house
And filled its every room;
A silent spirit haunting me
From dawn to dusky gloom.

★   ★   ★

I loved the house, I left the house,
I sold it all too soon;
The ghost that drove me from the house
Marked neither sun nor moon;

It never moved from out the house,
Was never there to see;
The ghost was all I dreaded most,
The ghost in the house was me.

Things were made worse by the fact that Eleanor herself was in no state to play her usual part of confidante. I could not burden her with my problems at that time. There is, however, one letter from her written in 1959, at the point when I had had to decide to cut my losses, put the studio back into Hamptons' hands and ask them to find a purchaser for me. This was an even worse moment than when, a year later, I left the house which I had built out of the studio and lived in for about six months. Because in the second case I had known such depression in the period after the house-warming that I was only too thankful to turn my back on the place and go.

On the earlier occasion, in 1959, Eleanor had not yet had the operation and was able to write me one of her loving and consoling letters.

Nov. 19th 1959

I am praying simply that you may be restored to normal health of body, mind and spirit, and able to go on quietly in your search for interior peace with Our Lord always behind you. You have had the shock of a great upheaval—not a great sorrow, as death can be, or a great danger, like sin, or the tragedy of broken friendships—but the shock of sudden complicated circumstances the effect of which shakes and bewilders, like a violent fall, a nature like yours. When the complications are settled no bones will have been broken, the effects will subside, and it will matter far less if you are a little poorer materially. What really matters materially is that you do not have to live by a sudden mistake. What matters in your spiritual and mental being is safe with Our Father, Our Lord and Our Lady. They see you helping them steadfastly if a little aridly. You will be eased, and better health will follow as 'Normalcy' succeeds the anxieties. If this ease can begin for you in the coming thirty days, how grateful I'll be. I think I was on the verge of knowing what small share I might have again in trying to help, but after 'Seclusion—Clausara' last night I knew for certain.

Now be quiet, darling, and not afraid.

The reference towards the end of her letter shows she must have been once more saying the Thirty Days Prayer for me.

However, my brief phase of being a householder and an inhabitant of Hampstead had taught me a great deal, and I was nothing but grateful to be able to return to being once more a mere week-end visitor up there at Eleanor's.

*

Whatever effect to the good these highly coloured happenings may have had on me, there is no doubt that Eleanor had begun to go downhill. She was by that time approaching her eightieth birthday. In addition to this she had had both of her eye operations and another lesser one in the Westminster Hospital. Following upon these, over the next year or two she had had a toe removed and finally another serious operation for gallstone, from which she might well have not recovered.

Highly successful though the two cataract operations were, under her beloved surgeon, Mr. H. B. Stallard, and though she found herself with sight such as she had never before experienced, yet Eleanor found it difficult for some time to adjust herself to this new vision. She had a feeling of seeing *too* much and too clearly. It distressed her and made her confused. In fact, to carry her over this interim period, she had to be given a special pair of glasses which would actually prevent her from seeing too distinctly.

All this strain and distress, to be followed later by the fifth operation in the Middlesex, drained her remaining strength and taxed even Eleanor's morale. During these years she certainly deteriorated physically, and became sadly conscious of failing faculties and the helplessness of old age. For the first time she found herself up against the plight that the aged experience in these days, when it is difficult to get things done and to find people to look after them.

How often I heard her say, "She was sweet; she was so *concerned* about me." 'Concerned' became a favourite word. Latterly Eleanor gave me the sad feeling that she was 'little Nellie' once again, crying for her mother and the consolations of that nursery in the nineties. "I want my boys," she cried out once to me in the winter of 1963, when she was very low in body and spirit. It was not like her, this *cri de coeur*, but it was inevitable that she should have these frequent downward swings towards the end of her life; and considering all she had been through in the way of illness she had many brighter periods of being the old courageous Eleanor, keeping her spirits up by her unselfishness and tremendous will power.

A long and wonderful letter, written during this very time, must be included here. It might be a help to many and shows yet once again Eleanor's power of taking trouble and thinking of others, even when life was becoming so much less happy for herself.

Palm Sunday, 1964

Yesterday evening was sweet for me, and after supper was wonderful. When I wasn't asleep last night I was thinking about it, and my thoughts of their own volition tried to shape themselves into things I would like to have said. One's night-thinking has moments when it says almost the right words—I mean "right" in the sense that they approach as near to what is true for oneself as one is able to come. Now having read the Palm Sunday Service quietly in bed, with a long restful day before me, I will try to say something I found words for, about two of the things we talked of, before I do anything else. Both have to do with Identity; first our own Identities, and then the Identity of Christ which you don't feel through the Bible— not because you never did, but because that source has been blunted by habitual familiarity. First, *our* Identities (especially yours).

You asked what I really feel about our after life in Heaven, whether I *really* felt we should be there with the people we've known and loved here. It is *really* impossible for me to feel anything else for the reason (yes, Reason *does* come into this for me) that whatever the life may be and however impossible to imagine, the conditions that apply to each of us after death *must* apply to all of us. And if you believe, as I do, that the identities we are born with accompany us into that after-life, theirs must also have accompanied them. By Identity I mean, not all those earthly burdens of Self we try to rid ourselves of, to purge ourselves of while we are living the life of the world, but the pure Persons that are Denys Blakelock, and Eleanor Farjeon; and our parents and brothers and sisters, and everyone we have known and loved (and have been indifferent to and hated). There won't be a separate, separated lot for each one of us, it will be the common lot to be united there—with all our differences—in the Mystical Body of Christ. Just as it is our common lot here to share so un-mystically and disunitedly the conditions of life imposed on all of us who are born into this imperfect world. It is impossible for me to believe that heavenly life is imperfect. What we suffer from here is the terrible struggle against the world's, and still more our own, imperfections. And when You, Denys Blakelock, are suffering most from this earthly struggle, what part of yourself is it that suffers most? Isn't it your Identity, borne down by your sense of sin and imperfection? Isn't it *You*? And isn't it this very You that is afraid of death, because it dreads what it may have to face in the after-life? And haven't all the You's, all the Persons you've ever known, had the same dreads and fears as part of the common conditions on earth? Whom else *can* you find in the after-life? If you can even imagine being alone in it, aren't you trying to picture a life for You individually, instead of a life which is shared by everyone who ever was, is, and will be? Only, it will be a perfect life, Denys, instead of an imperfect one. You can arrange individual conditions on earth for yourself as an Author, such conditions as *I've* never imagined in my seventy years of Authorship. But I don't think even Mr. Playgent can arrange individual conditions for your soul in Heaven. I mean conditions that exclude your friends. God has seen to that; He and Our Lord, and the Holy Spirit who resides in us as our share of Eternity. They have seen to that in pure Love. For men like you the fears and the suffering are far more in this life than the next. I, 'Eleanor Farjeon a Sinner', who speak without any authority but my unquenchable faith that the Trinity is Love, in which no speck of hate can exist, dare to say this to you on this Blessed Sunday in which, as I look out of my windows, my palm tree has flowered into golden blossom. I shall find you, or you will find me, in heaven presently, with everyone we long to find there, and all the others too. (The one exception, of course, is Queen Victoria: 'No! We will not know David.")

Now, Our Lord's Identity. When I first read (in my thirties) the Sermon on the Mount, it bowled me over; it was enough for me to want to live by. The impact was overwhelming. But I never thought of the Personality of the man who said it, I only knew and accepted that he was the Son of God. And that in itself was enough, when I had doubled my age, to make me feel I was not a hypocrite in going to Farm Street. But I did not continue to read and live by the Bible, or examine what I thought and felt about it; so that the sharp "edge of solemn pleasure" wasn't blunted for me by familiarity. And I now can't read His words (most of them) without feeling they are the truth which supports my faith. Not that this belief has perpetual power to lift me out of myself in my most difficult needs. But I have never been able to personify him; and if you realise how almost impossible it is for any one of us to convey to others the personality of people we've known who are dead and they can never meet humanly for themselves, then the task of Christ's Apostles and Disciples becomes tremendous. They conveyed what he said, and by *their* inspired faith convinced those who heard them. Those who caught faith from them and were baptised, thenceforth received themselves some direct impact of Our Lord through the Holy Spirit. But going back to the source of those few who actually knew him, they could only write down and report his actual words for the rest of us; and repetitive listening and reading can be deadened by habit, except for persons of perpetual spiritual awareness, which most of us aren't. If you and I had known him (as we know Father Benignus) we would, once in our lifetime, have received something that habit can't deaden; even if it can't *always* support us with its first impact of living light, we can recall it as something that did happen to us, once and for all. It was the love in Christ—who *was* Love—that the Gospels can't fully convey, while they record. St. John comes nearest to giving us the living, loving Son of Man who was God. It is that Man you long to find, isn't it? I can understand that you can feel and find him more positively in the writings of men who have found him and are your contemporaries, and can receive Christ's Identity afresh from them, when the far-away Gospellers who once helped you now fail you.

If I were writing this letter for publication, I'd have to work and work at it, and cut and re-write it for a week, before it could go into a nutshell and not be clogged with verbiage. If that is what it amounts to, tell yourself that it is written out of the deepest love in me to the deepest need in you; not even to comfort you, but perhaps to help you a little who help others so much more than you know, and purge yourself with suffering while you do it.

All the same, despite the concern for others and the spirit and vigour shown by this letter, there were disturbing times when Eleanor would reveal to me her fear that she was 'disintegrating' mentally. I used to tell her she must not even say such things; that there was abundant evidence in her activities that this was not true. I was proved to be right over and over again; for, long after she began to talk in that strain, she lived on to perform tasks of writing that would have been a tax on the mental powers of many people younger than herself.

Eleanor was always in poor shape physically from the first days of our meeting, because she neglected herself, as she neglected the plumbing and the electric fittings of her home. She disliked making appointments with specialists or with chiropodists, or having to answer the door to workmen who might come and disturb the things that to her really mattered like her writing. In consequence, she was inclined to wait till her feet could carry her no further, or the ball-cock refused to do its job, before she took the necessary steps to call the experts in.

But her fears were groundless. Mentally, Eleanor Farjeon was unimpaired if weary up to her last illness, which was of comparatively short duration. She was still proud of doing her Income Tax returns; and she continued to refuse the aid of accountants until, in 1965, she consented to put her financial affairs into the hands of Leslie Nash who had looked after our family for many years.

Eleanor liked figures and was very good at them; though because she was not conventionally educated I fancy her methods at arriving at her conclusions were irregular and would not have satisfied the educational authorities.

She had some trenchant things to say about the modern horrors of teaching children by machines and computers. I remember her saying that it was all of a piece with battery hens. This, too, was something she felt very strongly about; she wouldn't have any poor chicken near her table before satisfying herself as to its free and joyous rearing.

CHAPTER NINETEEN

ELEANOR'S EIGHTY-FOURTH BIRTHDAY fell on a Saturday. We had arranged that I should not go up to Hampstead
for the day itself, as she would be having many callers. I was
to join her on the Sunday as usual for luncheon, tea and
presents and stay till after supper. This sort of arrangement
had settled down into our weekly programme. She looked
forward to it and still insisted on arranging meals, even if they
had to be cooked beforehand. Eleanor liked to be able to do
that much, and she often said, "I enjoy getting down into my
kitchen again." I had always told her I was prepared to ter-
minate this arrangement at any time and to bring up picnic
meals, as she used to do for me at the beginning of our friendship, when she was still strong and active.

When I got up to Hampstead on this particular Sunday I
could see she had enjoyed her birthday and had been warmed
by the love and remembrances of so many friends, and by all
their gifts and greetings; but she said she was 'glad to have got
through it' and was very exhausted.

For three or four weeks she had been writing a Foreword
to a new collection for children of Edward Thomas's poems.
At that time she really was not fit for such a task, for as usual
she brought all her perfectionism to bear upon it. Eleanor
always gave full measure in her Forewords and she did no less
than eleven typings of this one, quite apart from her usual

long-hand manuscript. She had at last managed to get it done and posted to The Bodley Head the day before her birthday. The intense and prolonged concentration which this had demanded had reduced her to a state of vertigo and mental confusion.

When we were resting after luncheon as was our custom, she suddenly gave a little involuntary cry which went to my heart. When I expressed my concern and questioned her, she said, "You ought to go home." "I'm not going home," I said. Then she cried out despairingly, "I can't *bear* people to see me when I feel like this."

After a time I made tea and we had a long talk. I tried to console her by pointing out that she had been driving herself too hard and it was very natural that she should have brought about her present exhaustion. She said that, in addition to all that, she still was not completely satisfied with what she had written. As we talked she began to feel happier and then I asked her if she would like to read the Foreword to me. She said she would. When she came to speak it aloud to someone she could not but realise how good it was. It had the old magic; it was Eleanor Farjeon at her best. "No wonder you feel dizzy," I said.

She was pleased and stimulated by my immediate and obviously genuine reaction to the Foreword. After that we had a happy evening and I left her quite a different woman. Although Eleanor suffered from the many physical symptoms of old age she was a very emotional character. She could become quite ill through something that was troubling her unconsciously, as in this case of the Edward Thomas

Foreword. But the older she got the more she needed constant comfort and concern and the reassurances of those who loved her. I was determined that she should have them from me, remembering all that I had received from her.

For so much of my life I have leaned on other people. Never did I lean harder on anyone than I did on Eleanor Farjeon, and she took the full weight of the burdens that I carried. I little thought the day would come when I should be asked to take the weight of hers and find I had the strength to do it.

Eleanor had been a great carrier of other people's burdens; a great healer of other people's wounds. Now in the last years it was a case of 'Physician, heal thyself.' She had a hard struggle to apply to her own case all the wisdom that she had given to others. She was so stimulated by human contacts, so unselfish and so good at covering up, that I am sure many of the friends who came to see her would have been surprised, as well as distressed, if they had known how she could collapse after they had gone.

Because Eleanor had never been self-analytical she was therefore not good at explaining what she felt. But she did tell me, in that eighty-fourth birthday talk, that she felt the lack of someone who could 'assume responsibility'. She again spoke of a state of 'confusion' and a feeling of inability to deal with the practical and domestic side of things. But there was a great difficulty here. Eleanor should indeed by then have had someone living in, who would have run everything for her and seen to it that she had appetising little meals at the right moments. She ate next to nothing except at the week-end when I was there. But in order to enjoy this kind of care and immunity from responsibilities she would have had to give up that perfect freedom of her own rather Bohemian way of living that she had enjoyed for so many years and that was still so precious to her.

This was all very understandable, but it made her something of a problem for her family and friends as the years crept up on her. Fortunately she had long ago acquired the three-roomed cottage in Perrin's Court, less than five minutes away, and in that she had been able to install a series of people who lived there rent-free and received a small salary in return for varying degrees of services. At least they were on the telephone and could come over in an emergency. But the time had arrived by early 1965 when this was not really enough.

For that birthday I had found a Victorian card which delighted her, especially the verse printed on it. "I adore your card," she said as she read out the words; "It could hardly be more sentimental—or more restrained."

> Dear Friend, thy natal day recurring,
> These lines to thee I send,
> In all sincerity averring
> Kind wishes to my friend.
> And often may the task be mine
> Such days to celebrate,
> Each brighter than the former shine,
> And happier still thy fate.

Eleanor's sense of humour seldom failed her. Nor, however bad she might be feeling, could she ever be lacking in concern for others. Her immediate response, for instance, to a few words on the telephone from me about some family trouble:

March 11th 1965

Oh! I wish your lives—all three—need not be so clouded with sorrow.

You must never *not* speak of it to me, or feel you're over-grieving me. The sharing is what gives friendship its depth—the sharing, not the sparing. Share always.

And one day, not long after that birthday, I had this frag-mentary but touchingly expressive note in reply to a repeated assurance on my part that she could count on me to the end:

March 1st, 1965

We have just spoken and rung off, and as I laid down the receiver I heard myself saying, "Oh it's Everything—it's *everything*." It is, Denys. It is everything.

And this ending to a letter in which she had quoted a long passage from one she had received from her beloved Father Benignus in which he had written: 'St. Teresa of Avila used to say at the end of the day, "Thank God, another day nearer to Eternity." '

. . . whichever of us precedes the other into that 'ecstasy of happiness' forever (and it doesn't matter which of us it is) will wait there in the radiant certainty of the other's coming.

CHAPTER TWENTY

AFTER THE BIRTHDAY talk Eleanor made one of her amazing *risorgimentos*. But this time it was very temporary. For a short period, with her will she drove herself on to live as normal and active a life as possible within the confines of her own home. But very soon it became evident that she was entering a new phase. She began to develop many disquieting symptoms, and over the time it took for them to add up to something I fear she must have suffered intensely.

One morning in Easter week I had this letter enclosing a cheque:

April 19th, 1965

I feel as though I might soon be very very ill, but of course I may be wrong. However, in case I must go suddenly to hospital, and am not fit to arrange things, please bank this £100 and use it as needed for home expenses here, consulting Lilian and Elsie—up to £50.

And if I should die unexpectedly, please give Elsie and Lilian £25 each as a present, so they can have something to go on with. They are such dears. I'd like every consideration to be given to Lilian about the cottage. At the moment I can't try to plan anything. They'll do their best for Benny if I'm in hospital.

I daresay this is all nonsense.

The usual thought for others. Even at a time like this,

Eleanor thinks of the faithful Elsie Palmer who had come in to work for her day in, day out and had been her friend for many years. And she is concerned for Lilian and Tom Parker —Salvationists—who by then were living in the cottage and looking after her with as much tenderness as if she were their own. And of course Benny . . .

Early on the Saturday morning in Easter week Eleanor's doctor, Oliver Plowright, brought a second opinion to see her. The diagnosis was not an optimistic one. Whatever they told her or did not tell her, I am quite sure that Eleanor knew the nature of her illness and all that it might mean.

The next day I went to see her. I sat by her bedside and we had a short talk. Although nothing was made explicit about her complaint, she told me she was accepting the inevitable change in her way of life. This was a reference to the two things that mattered most to her: the surrender of her independence (as she must never be left alone now), and the end of her writing.

Considering all that this meant to her, she was wonderfully quiet and calm, and as usual uncomplaining. She even managed to laugh and make a joke or two.

The following morning Eleanor's parish priest, Canon Geraerts, came to administer the Sacrament of Extreme Unction. After that she was very peaceful. Although we were told that she might live for many years, there was somehow a feeling of finality and sadness in the air. But on the Thursday of that week suddenly the atmosphere changed. Her whole condition appeared to have improved. Once again she was taking telephone calls (in small doses) and scribbling little notes. I even received a large envelope, addressed in her normal handwriting, containing a muffler I had left behind. The doctor seemed hopeful that Eleanor might recover perhaps eighty per cent of her former health.

It made a great difference to her to feel that so many people whom she loved and who loved her were rallying round to do their share of looking after her. Especially the members of her own family.

One episode particularly touched her. Paul, the gardener, who was a Dane and devoted to Eleanor, went up to her room and held her hands for a moment between his own great horny ones. Later, in the street, he met her nurse. "Do not let my Miss Ellen die," he said in his Danish accent, "I do not let my flowers die."

The love and the natural poetry of this made a very special appeal to Eleanor's heart.

She did not fulfil our hopes of her recovery. She died on June 5th, the Eve of Whitsun.

Eleanor Farjeon would not, I am sure, have wished me to dwell on the sadness of those few weeks of early summer when her spirit began to leave us.

I saw her every day for a few moments in that final week and she always recognised me until the last two days. Although she spoke with much difficulty, on June 3rd she made it plain that she knew the end had come. We spoke of the friendship we had had and said that that would go on for always. It is doubtful how plainly she could see, but quite suddenly she looked up at me intently and said, "You won't grieve, will you?"

Even then, at that moment of mental confusion, physical weakness and distress, Eleanor's natural habit of unselfishness asserted itself, and she could think of me, as she had done at our first strange meeting fifteen years before.

*

In writing this Memoir, I have tried to keep faithfully to my original intention: that it should be a picture of Eleanor Farjeon and not an account of my own life. Nevertheless, as I have gone on writing, I have been conscious of the difficulty of not bringing myself in over much. Because Eleanor Farjeon's life was so closely bound up with mine for that last long phase, if I were to paint a true picture of her it seemed to become increasingly impracticable to keep myself to any real extent in the background. Character is shown most plainly through incident, and through the impact of the person under review on those who have lived nearest to that person. This seems particularly true of Eleanor Farjeon, a character so idiorhythmic, so complex, so many-sided and diverse.

If to those legion who knew and loved her I have presented a portrait which they can recognise and take pleasure from, in remembering the Eleanor they knew; and if for those readers who admired her work, and through it loved the writer, I have been able to bring her a little closer, and make them feel that to them she is now something more than just a favourite author, then I have succeeded in my task.

*

At the end of our holiday in Cornwall back in 1951, Eleanor

wrote for me the poem which I treasure most. I have pur-
posely not included it before. Just as it made a touching
termination to all that that holiday had meant to us, so it
seems to me now to have its fitting place in the finale of this
book.

For D.B. June 3rd, 1951

Do not be sad for a time that seems swiftly ended.
Nothing can end
Days that have been so perfectly befriended
By friend and friend.
For their perfection was neither of time nor of place,
Nor of any weather
Or mood that brightened or shadowed this little space
Of being together.
It has been a cupful of time dipped out of an endless
Sea: it has been
A handful of earth that might have been fruitless and
  friendless,
And love made green.
What was begun in time and place is unfinished;
There is no end,
And the sea is unemptied, the earth is undiminished
For friend and friend.

★

The book shall finish as it began—but with a difference:
  "Harry-Nellie-Joe-and-Bertie . . . Bertie died first, didn't
he?"

"Yes, in 1945. We buried him on V Day . . . Harry in 1948, and Joe in 1955."

"And then there was one." I held my hand out to Eleanor across the kitchen table where we always fed. She took it and said, "Yes, but, like Wordsworth's child, I still say, *We are four.*"

Nellie died in 1965. And then there were none. . . . ? All the same, I seem even now to hear Eleanor's voice replying firmly, "No. But, like Wordsworth's child, I still say, *We are four.*"